W9-BCD-778

Contents

READY, SET,

THE KINESTHETIC CLASSROOM 2.0

GO!

I would like to dedicate this book to Wendy Miller, principal at the outstanding Challenge Charter School in Glendale, Arizona; to the Bower Foundation and the Office of Healthy Schools at The Mississippi Department of Education; and especially to Anne, Dale, Mary Ann, and Shane, who first gave wings to my voice.

Mike Kuczala

My devoted mother taught me to believe in myself, set my goals high, and reach for the stars. M.B.P shares with me an unconditional love that motivates me to grow and give everything I have. My dedicated family provides me with endless support and respect. My loyal friends inspire me to smile and enjoy the simple things in life. This book is dedicated to these special people who fill me with joy, love, and happiness every day. I can't imagine where I would be without them. I sincerely thank each one of them for their tireless encouragement in helping me become the person I am today.

Traci Lengel

READY, SET,

THE KINESTHETIC CLASSROOM 2.0

GO!

MIKE KUCZALA

TRACI LENGEL

FOREWORD BY PAUL ZIENTARSKI

A Joint Publication

CORWIN
A SAGE Publishing Company

KIDSFIT™

FOR INFORMATION:

Corwin
A SAGE Company
2455 Teller Road
Thousand Oaks, California 91320
(800) 233-9936
www.corwin.com

SAGE Publications Ltd.
1 Oliver's Yard
55 City Road
London, EC1Y 1SP
United Kingdom

SAGE Publications India Pvt. Ltd.
B 1/I 1 Mohan Cooperative Industrial Area
Mathura Road, New Delhi 110 044
India

SAGE Publications Asia-Pacific Pte. Ltd.
3 Church Street
#10-04 Samsung Hub
Singapore 049483

Program Director: Jessica Allan
Senior Associate Editor: Kimberly Greenberg
Senior Editorial Assistant: Katie Crilley
Marketing Manager: Anna Mesick
Production Editor: Veronica Stapleton Hooper
Copy Editor: Pam Schroeder
Typesetter: Hurix Systems Pvt. Ltd.
Proofreader: Ellen Howard
Indexer: Karen Wiley
Cover Designer: Scott Van Atta

This book is printed on acid-free paper.

Certified Chain of Custody
Promoting Sustainable Forestry
www.sfiprogram.org
SFI-01268

SFI label applies to text stock

17 18 19 20 21 10 9 8 7 6 5 4 3 2 1

Foreword

Do not train a child to learn with force or harshness, but direct them to it by what amuses their minds, so that you may be better able to discover with accuracy the peculiar bent of genius of each.

—Plato (BC 477–BC 347), Greek philosopher

Even Plato knew that children will learn only when movement amuses the mind. Teachers become frustrated when they teach information that students find boring and uninteresting based on content, assessment, and accountability. They feel they have no time to incorporate kinesthetic learning. Research shows that students do not remember facts and concepts that are uninteresting. Therein lies the disconnect. Mike Kuczala and Traci Lengel have incorporated ideas that enable teachers to think outside the box in terms of how instruction is delivered. They provide a broad array of how to use movement to teach kinesthetically. It is their belief, and mine as well, that the examples contained in this book will enhance student engagement and thereby improve student learning.

Research shows that 85 percent of people are kinesthetic learners. In my own experience, students scored 20 percent higher on a quiz when they read while riding an exercise bike as opposed to sitting at a desk. Some of the teaching staff applied kinesthetic concepts in our high school at Naperville Central in Illinois. We put students in a physical education class prior to classes in which they struggled. Academic teachers in reading improvement and algebra readiness made a concerted effort to incorporate movement in their classes. The reading teachers even allowed students to ride exercise bikes while reading their assignments. The data we collected proved that all of these interventions were quite valuable and the improvement in student growth was phenomenal. More importantly the students have become staunch supporters of the program. When asked to give testimony to the visiting educators—who have come from 26 states and eight foreign countries—they unanimously agree that they have learned more and thus improved their test scores as a result of the structure of the classes. The teachers have been delightfully amazed at student progress.

Mike and Traci have referenced noted neuroscientists to confirm their work. By highlighting the work of Dr. John Ratey, Dr. John Medina, Eric

Jensen, Dr. Carla Hannaford, and noted movement expert Jean Blaydes Moize, they bring true validity to their work of understanding the value of adding movement to the classroom. Using movement to enhance learning is the key to their concepts. Neuroscience studies now show that getting students out of their desks helps with an overall feeling of well-being. Adding exercise to the classroom alters the neurochemicals in the brain. This helps relieve stress and anxiety, improves attention, and can aid in the childhood epidemic of obesity our country is facing.

I'm familiar with their first book, *The Kinesthetic Classroom: Teaching and Learning Through Movement*. I often reference the book when doing my work as an educational consultant. The examples they give for classroom activities encompass subject matters in all curricular areas including language arts, math, science, social studies, art, and music. All teachers can look at those examples and apply them to their classrooms and curriculums. This book adds even more ideas to their first, so utilizing both books vastly increases a teacher's repertoire.

I believe one of the biggest benefits of this book is that it encourages teachers to engage their students in activities that involve not only learning academics but also interactive social skills. In the modern age, when people are so connected to their cell phones and other technology, it is imperative that schools teach students how to engage with each other. Businesses want intelligent employees who can work cooperatively with others and show the necessary social skills to be productive workers and team players.

This book will prove to be an invaluable tool to the experienced teachers looking to improve their skills or even to reinvent themselves after years of doing the same old thing. It is also critical for new teachers as they venture into their profession, arming them with tools to aid in student engagement and learning.

—*Paul Zientarski*
Retired Department Chairman and Learning Readiness
PE Coordinator Naperville Central High School
PE/Educational Consultant

Preface

Learning doesn't happen from the neck up;
it happens from the feet up.

—Mike Kuczala

There's a trainer we know, a former member of the United States Marine Corps. Just that information alone should tell you what his workouts are like: tough, inventive, disciplined, challenging, and most of all, exhausting. Continued movement is a cornerstone; rest is rare. These group training sessions are not for the faint of heart. A mix of running, crawling, jumping, lunging, hopping, lifting, swinging, being inside and out, make you crave the comfort of your car ride home. He does not let up on you. He is motivating and encouraging and occasionally will get in your face to make sure you are not letting up on yourself, even for a moment. There is a hum to the class as he moves around the gym barking instructions in his uniquely Marine way that gets you to do just a little more.

Chris Kaag is quite accomplished. After his retirement from the Marine Corps, he earned a business degree from Pennsylvania State University and shortly thereafter started his own business, Corps Fitness—out of the back of his truck. His experience in the Marines and his mental toughness started him down a path that would eventually inspire thousands of people to get in the best shape of their lives. He had no physical gym to bring his participants to when he first started. Chris had members of his class running steps and low crawling through sand pits in various parks in the local area. His business grew and eventually moved indoors. In 2007 he started the IM ABLE Foundation. Today, Chris has built one of the most dominant and popular places of fitness in Berks County, Pennsylvania, where he also enjoys a board room and enough office space to run IM ABLE. He advocates living life to the fullest with no excuses. He inspires others to realize their potential and will do anything to help them reach it. The Corps Fitness community prides itself on respect, accountability, and teamwork. Corps Fitness provides a space where people can push themselves, redefine their fitness limits, and in the process develop a can-do attitude. Chris inspires others to become the best they can be—physically and emotionally.

What is the IM ABLE Foundation? It was created to build and support active lifestyles for individuals with disabilities, currently known as different abilities. Chris Kaag, the inspiration to so many and founder of Corps Fitness, operates from a wheelchair. You read that correctly. This inspirational human being and former Marine gets in your face from his self-propelled moveable chair. He lives with a neurodegenerative condition known as adrenomyeloneuropathy, which started with a concussion during his second tour of duty in Aviano, Italy. In 1999 he was medically retired from the Marine Corps, holding the rank of sergeant. Upon receiving his diagnoses, Chris had a decision to make. He could either give up and let his condition control his life or dig deep and push on. You know what he chose and how the story is currently playing out.

At its very core, Chris understands that a life worth living includes being physical; we are meant and built to move, be physically active, and be physically fit. He sets an example by living his life with a different ability that would stunt many; but he still drives, skis, and krankcycles all over the place! He is in phenomenal shape, and if he can achieve that, anyone can! He is an inspiration and example of a physical life well lived. He is an inspiration to us. *Ready, Set, Go: The Kinesthetic Classroom 2.0* takes from that inspiration and testifies to a physical life in education. No child or young adult should ever have to endure his or her experience of learning and discovery mostly from a seat.

Ready, Set, Go: The Kinesthetic Classroom 2.0 is a resource that provides all teachers, in every content area and grade level, with a quick means to finding information and ideas on how to implement thoughtful and purposeful movement and physical activity in the classroom to enhance the teaching and learning process. It supports the notion of educating the child as a whole. The suggested activities all provide opportunity for students to grow cognitively, socially, mentally, emotionally, and physically. Four distinct purposes for using movement in the classroom will be shared. Although the framework is similar to the one we introduced in *The Kinesthetic Classroom: Teaching and Learning Through Movement,* we've reshaped the flow and sequence as follows:

TAKE YOUR POSITION!

Gain knowledge
Know the research
Recognize the benefits

Ready!

Devise a plan
Create cohesion

Set!

Prepare the brain
Provide brain breaks (or boosts, blasts, etc.)
Fitness challenges

Go!

Review content
Teach content

The sequential steps in this framework are supported by cutting-edge educational research explaining the benefits of using movement as a method in the teaching and learning process. This book will serve as a critical tool for delivering content and curriculum to teachers and students, all while using a brain-friendly approach. We hope that you allow this framework to become the standard for using kinesthetic activities and movement to support and enhance curriculum objectives. These activities should be included in all classrooms that are committed to engaging the learner and differentiation instruction.

Chapter 1 discusses both the modern learner and transforming the learning environment through taking your position and becoming a kinesthetic educator. The four purposes of movement and the research supporting each provide a direct route to combat the current educational and health concerns of children. An extensive graphic organizer explains "Ready, Set, Go: Framework 2.0" including these purposes. The framework allows for teachers to progress in the implementation of movement at their own pace. Teachers' comfort levels regarding movement in the classroom may vary greatly. In this chapter, guidance is provided at a pace that is individualized.

Classrooms, schools, and school districts have changed with regard to movement, physical activity, and physical education since the publication of the original Kinesthetic Classroom. Chapter 2 discusses how classrooms and schools have evolved and includes the research that continues to support the use of classroom physical activity. This chapter also describes some unique success stories around the United States as well as the emergence of Action Based Learning Labs and kinesthetic classroom furniture.

Through nine phrases, or thoughts, Chapter 3 describes how the brain/body connection plays out in the classroom. The relationship between how the brain prefers to learn and the role movement plays in this process is closely examined. Presenting information on the brain/body connection through these statements makes the information more applicable for classroom teachers as they make decisions about how best to approach the teaching and learning process.

One serious concern regarding movement is classroom management. Chapter 4 is dedicated to this concern. It addresses building a kinesthetic classroom environment, safety, ease of movement, introducing movement, the unmotivated student, the hypermotivated student, and transfer time from movement to seat. Tips and strategies will be shared to better manage student behavior during movement activities.

Chapters 5 through 10 are action-packed with hundreds of movement activities that can be implemented in the classroom. Each chapter focuses on the other purposes of movement. Suggestions are easy to follow and practical. Movement activities are appropriate for various grade, fitness, and ability levels. Recommendations are made on how to adapt and customize certain activities. Usually, little or no equipment is needed.

Chapter 5 addresses the importance of building a classroom environment through class cohesion. Although these activities are not intended for daily use, they serve a critical role. Students who feel safe and comfortable in a learning environment are more capable of optimal learning. Therefore, allowing students the opportunity to engage in these activities is advantageous to the learning process.

Chapters 6 through 8 focus on initiating movement in the classroom. These activities can be performed in two minutes or less. In fact, the challenges presented take only 30 or 60 seconds to complete. This is a perfect place for the cautious teacher to begin. Planning is minimal, and little time is taken away from academic content. These activities are great for reenergizing the body and brain while enhancing neural connections. After participating in these activities, the brain refocuses, and learning becomes more efficient.

Chapters 9 and 10 concentrate on curriculum. These activities, which include music, art, and health, are designed to expose teachers to a different way of thinking. To teach and review content through movement, teachers must be willing to stray from traditional teaching techniques. Many of these movement activities are intended to supplement teaching methods already being used. Sometimes, a suggested activity may actually replace a current teaching practice. Either way, students are learning and reviewing academic content through exciting and stimulating means.

For more information on Chris Kaag and Corps Fitness, please visit www.corpsfitness.net.

Acknowledgments

Mike Kuczala

Paul Zientarski for writing the foreword and being a leader in such an important field.

Jessica Allan and Katie Crilley for their guidance and patience in writing this book.

Jean Blaydes Moize for her constant friendship, insight, encouragement, mentorship, and being willing to contribute to this book.

Cindy Hess, Dave Spurlock, David Genova, and Kelley Sullivan for being leaders in the field and contributing their passion to this book.

Ed Pinney and his team at Kidsfit for his friendship, mission, and making schools and classrooms better places to learn.

Andy Vasily, Jorge Rodriguez, Justin Schleider, Bob Knipe, Andrew Milne, Nicholas Endlich, and David Gusitsch for their continued support and cheerleading and caring the way they do about the future of our children.

All of my colleagues at Regional Training Center. Coming across that brochure all those years ago changed everything.

Traci Lengel

Heather Anthony for her endless patience, strength, support, and inspiration.

Sue Rose, Michelle Vuono, Michaela Zajicova, Toni Pratt, Mark Bartkowski, Robyn Patrick, and Heidi Donohue for their friendship, insight, and collaboration.

Tina Satterwhite, Trisha Backes, Tammy Bachert, Todd Anthony, and Jason Anthony for their love and encouragement.

Jenna Evans for challenging me intellectually and lighting the way as I strengthen my vision; her creative thinking, collaboration, and friendship are invaluable.

Lee Anthony for his dedication, commitment, and love.

Emma and Alivia Backes for their smiles, hugs, and participation.

Cathy Zavacki for her contributions in science, Phillip Hochman for social studies, and Carrie Kizuka for math. These three educators are innovative, brilliant, and leaders in their fields.

All the amazing, creative students who have helped us shape and develop our teaching methodologies.

All the educators who have experienced our graduate courses, workshops, presentations, and in-services. You have no idea how much we have learned and grown from you! We thank you for putting knowledge to work in the classroom.

About the Authors

Mike Kuczala is the coauthor of the Corwin Bestseller and Association of Educational Publishers' Distinguished Achievement Award-nominated *The Kinesthetic Classroom: Teaching and Learning Through Movement,* a book and philosophy that has changed views of teaching and learning around the world. Mike's second book, *Training in Motion: How to Use Movement to Create an Engaging and Effective Learning Environment,* was released in 2015 (AMACOM). President of Kuczala Consulting and academic director for the Regional Training Center, an educational consulting firm based in Randolph, New Jersey, Mike has become an in-demand keynote speaker and consultant at international conferences, school districts, and corporations. His standing-room-only presentations have been experienced in diverse settings such as the East Asia Regional Council of Schools; the American Society for Training and Development; the Forum for Innovative Leadership; the Association for Supervision and Curriculum Development; the American Association for Health, Physical Education, Recreation and Dance; and the Lawyer Brain OD Roundtable.

An expert in training, training design, and effective presentation, he has designed or codesigned four of the most successful graduate courses in the history of the Regional Training Center. Motivation: The Art and Science of Inspiring Classroom Success, Wellness: Creating Health and Balance in the Classroom, The Kinesthetic Classroom: Teaching and Learning Through Movement, and The Kinesthetic Classroom II: Moving Across the Standards are facilitated by a cadre of more than 70 trained instructors who have taught thousands of teachers the key principles of instructional movement, motivation, and wellness.

As a graduate instructor, keynote speaker, and workshop presenter, Mike regularly facilitates professional development programs in both corporate and educational settings in the areas of motivation, presentation skill, use of movement to enhance the learning process, brain-based teaching and training, differentiated instruction and training, enhancement of student thinking, and topics related to wellness and stress management. His engaging and practical professional development programs have been enjoyed by tens of thousands of teachers, administrators, corporate executives, and parents around the world during the last decade.

For more information, please visit his website at www.mikekuczala .com.

 **Traci Lengel** is a health and physical education teacher in the Pocono Mountain School District. With more than 25 years of experience, Traci's knowledge in movement education, motor development, life-long fitness/wellness, health education, curriculum development, and educational publication has contributed to the success of her insightful programs. Additionally, Traci is an adjunct professor at La Salle University in Pennsylvania and the College of New Jersey. In conjunction with these positions, she is a designer/coauthor of three graduate courses with Mike Kuczala. These highly esteemed graduate courses, titled Wellness: Creating Health and Balance in the Classroom; The Kinesthetic Classroom: Teaching and Learning Through Movement; and The Kinesthetic Classroom II: Moving Across the Curriculum have had a profound effect on the personal and professional lives of thousands of educators. Furthermore, Traci is coauthor of the book *The Kinesthetic Classroom: Teaching and Learning Through Movement,* which was published in 2010 and is widely known as a best-selling educational publication.

Known for her enthusiasm, innovation, work ethic, and passion, Traci devotes much of her time to both her personal and professional successes. With her motivational teaching methodology, she presents and facilitates workshops and provides keynote presentations for development programs in the areas of wellness, stress management, and teaching and learning through movement. Her ultimate professional challenge is to inspire educators at all levels to incorporate movement into their daily teaching. Traci's greatest joy is the unconditional love and support she shares with her family and friends. She is kindhearted and committed to bringing fun and laughter to education and the people who share her journey. Traci is persistent and dedicated and leaves a lasting impression. She can be reached at tlengel@pmsd.org.

PART 1

TAKE YOUR POSITION

Becoming a Kinesthetic Educator

1

Framework 2.0

THE EDUCATIONAL RACE: ARE WE WINNING?

The education of our youth will always be a well-analyzed and discussed topic in our society. Countries compare achievement and standardized test scores while examining curricula, daily schedules, and the accomplishments of the masses based on attainment and success. This debatable topic is perpetually scrutinized and displays evidence that supports both strengths and weaknesses in our current status as well as the future direction of today's educational system. However, the most important question we may ask ourselves is this: What exactly are we analyzing? Are students more intelligent now than our previous graduates? Are they more successful? What measurements are we using to determine this success? Moreover, is education playing a role in producing healthy, productive humanitarians who care about one another and the world we live in?

Strengths

Although some may argue the quality of today's educators, it is undeniable that teachers' responsibilities have grown tremendously to accommodate changes in society. Reading, writing, and arithmetic account only for a small aspect of educating our future generations. Today's classroom teacher has to differentiate instruction for each student as a unique individual learner while reaching and/or exceeding academic standards. Instruction and teaching methodologies are closely examined to improve standardized test scores. Modifications and varied assessments are explored to provide for optimal learning and achievement. To accomplish this wish list, teachers must be masterful at reaching academic as well as nonacademic needs of learners. Educators must now teach communication and decision-making skills, conflict resolution, and behavior management all while considering the health and well-being of their students. Today's teachers are highly educated prior to entering their careers. This education continues throughout their profession and includes a wide scope of expertise and knowledge. The well-rounded educator of the 21st century is an asset to the challenges of educating today's youth.

Another considerable strength of the educational system is the increase in postsecondary education. We currently have what is arguably the most rigorous curriculum in history, and yet graduation rates have still continued to increase. Students are experiencing academic success and are motivated to expand their knowledge through higher educational opportunities. Research has suggested that students are growing in intelligence at younger ages, and test scores are improving. This allows for the hopeful outlook that we are winning the educational race.

One of the most notable improvements in the educational system is the inclusion of all learners. Today's classroom provides the least restrictive environment for a variety of students. Individual needs are analyzed and addressed with the intention of each student reaching his or her full potential. This mentality has led the way to initiating a variety of programs that many believe have improved content standards and measurements. Today education serves all learners with the attitude that everyone can succeed.

Over time, education has shown many improvements that may lead some to believe that we are winning the educational race. The attention to trends, future expectations, and aspirations is persistent. As previously noted, more students are graduating and seeking posteducational experiences. Students are increasing their intelligence at a younger age, and a variety of programs exist to allow learners to reach their full potential. However, it's inevitable that we ask the question: Where is education failing our youth, and what might keep us from winning this daunting race?

Weaknesses

It can be difficult to face the problems our society is currently battling and consider that education may be playing a role in their development. However, there has been a clear, irrefutable pattern in the decline in the physical health and well-being of our youth. The obesity epidemic has caused detrimental effects to our younger generation. Are we now raising the first generation of children that may not outlive their parents? Many experts believe we are doing just that as the rapid and steady increase in type 2 diabetes and obesity may lead to many premature health diseases and illnesses. The youth brain is drawn to the seduction of technology. Children and young adults are consumed with internet, television, and social media. Their precious time is spent in a seated position, while their eyes are fixated on a screen for hours on end.

Sitting for long periods of time causes serious health risks such as weakened muscles and bones, increased blood pressure, a decrease in insulin effectiveness, burning fewer calories (which may lead to obesity), an increase in type 2 diabetes and certain cancers, a decrease in the body's ability to clean its blood, and a shorter life span (Hamilton, 2008). The home life and family structure for the younger generation is far less physically active than previous generations. Taking this into consideration, it is important to consider what our current educational system is doing to combat the war on obesity and the destruction of the younger generation's health and well-being. It's admirable that our students are getting smarter at much younger ages; however, if their health is compromised, we must consider if our priorities are in line with what's in the best interests of our future leaders.

A second serious concern of our youth today is the decline in social skills and behaviors. How do students speak to one another on a regular basis? Most conversations between younger people today take place through text messages and social media. In some instances this may be a positive occurrence for students who are shy or struggling with communication skills. However, are we now creating more people with communication challenges? Younger age people are still developing their interpersonal skills. The idea of actually speaking to someone in a phone conversation is decreasing at alarming rates. According to a Pew Institute survey, the number of text messages sent monthly in the United States exploded from 14 billion in 2000 to 188 billion in 2010 (Kluger, 2012). Is there an end in sight to this epidemic, or do you see these statistics increasing? How will this affect our future leaders?

What programs or goals are in place in today's educational system to contest the decline of our students' interpersonal skills? Have we developed student outcomes that focus on these crucial life skills, and are we measuring and encouraging them to the same extent that we do our academic standards? If students are not able to have appropriate, meaningful conversations with others, how will that affect the future success of our nation? Many people believe one of the biggest concerns with our youth is their expectation to get what they want, even in situations where they may not have earned it. Additionally, this era is known to many as "the age of entitlement." Are we giving in to student wants in a way that is crippling their work ethic and willingness to accept mediocrity?

Another important consideration of education today is the mental health of children. Mental health is a fundamental factor in a student's ability to learn, grow, and lead a productive life. While mental health services currently do not meet the needs of children, what are school systems doing to close this gap? One in five children has a diagnosable mental disorder, while one in 10 has a serious mental health problem that may impair how he or she functions in the home, school, and community (Stagman & Cooper, 2010). These statistics seem to be growing at steady rates.

Low self-esteem is a mental disorder in which an individual views himself or herself as inadequate, unworthy, or unloved. Many experts believe that low self-esteem is at an all-time high. Today's society, with social media at the forefront, leaves teens and youth feeling insufficient and depressed. Although this may not seem like a problem for the school setting, how can students perform at their full potential if they are struggling with feelings of incompetence on a consistent basis? It seems impossible for students to reach optimal levels of performance if they are struggling with low self-esteem, depression, or anxiety. This matter may not have been a leading concern with former educational strategies and policies, but to overlook it today would be negligent.

To win the educational race, a sole focus on student cognition may leave us short of the finish line. A comprehensive approach that includes cognition along with the physical, social, and mental/emotional well-being of our youthful society is an all-encompassing tactic that may produce a first place victory. It seems too simple to suggest that daily movement throughout the school day may play a significant role in helping win this race. Nonetheless, we are proposing just that; a kinesthetic classroom in conjunction with other successfully proven teaching methodologies will have a powerful impact on this never-ending challenge while pushing us ahead to triumph.

WHEN IS IT TIME TO TAKE MY POSITION AND BECOME A KINESTHETIC EDUCATOR?

Part 1: Take Your Position—Become a Kinesthetic Educator

The time to become a Kinesthetic Educator is now! You no longer have to wonder if it's in your students' best interest to incorporate movement activities into everyday teaching strategies. If you are not already doing so, take your position today, and decide to start and/or continue to teach kinesthetically on a regular, consistent basis. This teaching methodology will allow for optimal learning in your classroom environment. Movement in an academic setting allows for a stimulating, novel experience that attracts the youthful brain. Similar to the seduction of technology, the brain is drawn to the excitement and innovation that movement brings. Movement also provides the opportunity for students to grow cognitively, physically, socially, and mentally/emotionally. As educators use movement to enhance the learning process, academic standards can be met, test scores can continue to be improved, and vital life skills can be developed.

Technology has many positive aspects in today's society and has played a crucial role in the growth of our nation. However, many believe that spending too much time watching television, playing video games, surfing the internet, or exploring social media can have a detrimental effect on our lives, including our attention spans. Children who are raised in stimulating, active environments produce more neural connections in the brain (Bruer, 1991). When the body is inactive for 20 minutes or longer, there is a decline in neural communication (Kinoshita, 1997). Researchers at the University of Illinois found a "meaningful difference" in reading, spelling, and math achievement tests following exercise (Mitchell, 2009). It stands to reason that adding movement to the educational environment in conjunction with technology provides students with a win-win approach to optimize learning success and achievement.

As we previously analyzed our educational strengths and weaknesses, it is clear that teaching kinesthetically may play a key role in elevating our strengths while building on what many believe to be detrimental weaknesses. Research suggests that physically fit children perform better in the classroom. Research also shows a correlation between academic skills and physical fitness scores (Ratey, 2008). Recent studies surmise that physically fit students perform better on standardized test scores. Hence, teaching through kinesthetic means habitually could continue to increase these test scores along with performance standards.

Taking the position to become a Kinesthetic Educator will also help improve student retention. Movement should be considered whenever teaching a new concept or standard. Using kinesthetic activities and physical movement in the learning process will aide in students' abilities to recall information more efficiently (Blaydes Madigan, 1999). This will improve retention on a short- and long-term basis, which may result in colossal benefits. Today's curriculums are rigorous and have a spiral, sequential method that requires superlative retention.

It has been suggested that 80–85 percent of students are predominantly kinesthetic learners, which means they rely on kinesthetic intelligence for learning. This is an astronomical statistic that can no longer be ignored. In other words, these children prefer to move their bodies while participating in the learning process. Taking the position of becoming a Kinesthetic Educator will meet the needs of a variety of learners in your classroom because movement allows for a multimodality approach to teaching. In a time when the variety of learners is unlike ever before, it is imperative to grasp tools that can provide a diverse approach to various needs.

The physical benefits of movement have been known to our society for decades. It is common to read or hear about the value of leading an active lifestyle on a daily basis. The more we move our bodies, the better it is for our health and well-being. If our society is so clear on this phenomenon, it only makes sense to move students as often as we can to combat the physical concerns that plague our youth. It is a realistic connection to take the position to become a Kinesthetic Educator who uses movement in the classroom daily to help battle obesity and the other health risks of our future leaders. Movement is essential for healthy living; therefore, why would we want students sitting all day as opposed to moving, learning, and growing in a succinct effort to give the younger generation the best chance of success? If students are in an educational environment for a minimum of six hours a day, imagine the impact a Kinesthetic Educator can make on improving their students' physical health. However, also consider the opposing physical effects of sitting most of those school hours and the harm that may cause the health of our youth. The potential remedy seems without debate.

In conjunction to improving physical health, are there social benefits to providing movement activities in an academic environment on a consistent basis? Think back to when you were a child or young adult. Remember playing sports on a unified team or simple games of backyard tag? For these events to run smoothly, children needed to communicate effectively while agreeing on rules and guidelines for the games. Communication and problem solving skills were developed in every single game that was played. Now, imagine movement activities in a classroom setting. How would students need to communicate with one another to meet collaborative objectives successfully? Would interpersonal skills have the opportunity to be developed in these types of activities? Many movement activities allow for effective nonverbal and verbal communication for task goals to be met productively. Hence, a Kinesthetic Educator would enhance social skills along with academic achievement in an environment that supports teamwork, collaboration, and appreciation of individual differences through movement experiences.

The mental/emotional benefits of movement are continually praised in today's society. According to KidsHealth (2015), people who exercise regularly feel happier than people who do not. Exercise and movement can reduce anxiety and depression. Let's face it: when we move, we just feel better. Movement can improve self-confidence and self-esteem, which may result in an overall feel-good attitude. If teachers are moving students frequently throughout the day, students may enjoy the day more as the brain releases serotonin and adrenalin to aide in a better state of mind, which can enhance the learning process. Exercise is also used to help balance various mental health disorders. The chemicals released during movement activities may result in positive thinking and mental acuteness.

As we'll discuss in more depth later in the book, a student's learning state has a great influence on the meaning that is created during the learning process (Jensen, 2000). Therefore if a student has a positive learning state when material is being taught, the learner has an increased opportunity to make connections and better understand the concepts and information they are learning. Movement is the most powerful manager of a student's learning state (Jensen 2000). If an educator uses movement to teach academic standards, there is an opportunity for improved mental health challenges in students. If becoming a Kinesthetic Educator can improve self-esteem, reduce stress and depression, and enhance positivity, why wouldn't we embrace movement in an educational environment?

The educational setting is a constant in a student's life that our society has the ability to regulate based on public needs and objectives. It is difficult to manage what happens in home environments and how children and young adults optimize their time. However, we can have direct management of what happens throughout the school day. Taking the position of becoming a Kinesthetic Educator does not throw out all the other aspects of education that have proven successful. This movement expert simply adds kinesthetic activities into the daily routines of the school day in addition to the successful methodologies already in use. These movement activities can be used to enhance academic standards, improve test scores, and heighten intelligence and achievement, all while enriching the physical, social, and mental/emotional growth and well-being of our younger generation. A well-thought, comprehensive plan is underway to winning the educational race. The end result may not only be more intelligent children and young adults but perhaps, more importantly, humanitarians who seek to improve their own lives in conjunction with the world around them.

WHAT IS READY, SET, GO: FRAMEWORK 2.0?

Part 1: Take Your Position—Become a Kinesthetic Educator

Part 1 of the framework is deciding to take the position of becoming a Kinesthetic Educator. In this phase, educators gain knowledge and develop a philosophy of how movement will best serve their classroom and student needs. An essential part of this process is to grasp a clear understanding of the Framework 2.0 and how it can be used effectively to boost academic success along with the enjoyment of learning. This movement framework includes three additional parts that follow "Take your Position." These three sections are referred to as "Ready," "Set," and "Go."

Figure 1.1 Movement With Purpose: Framework 2.0

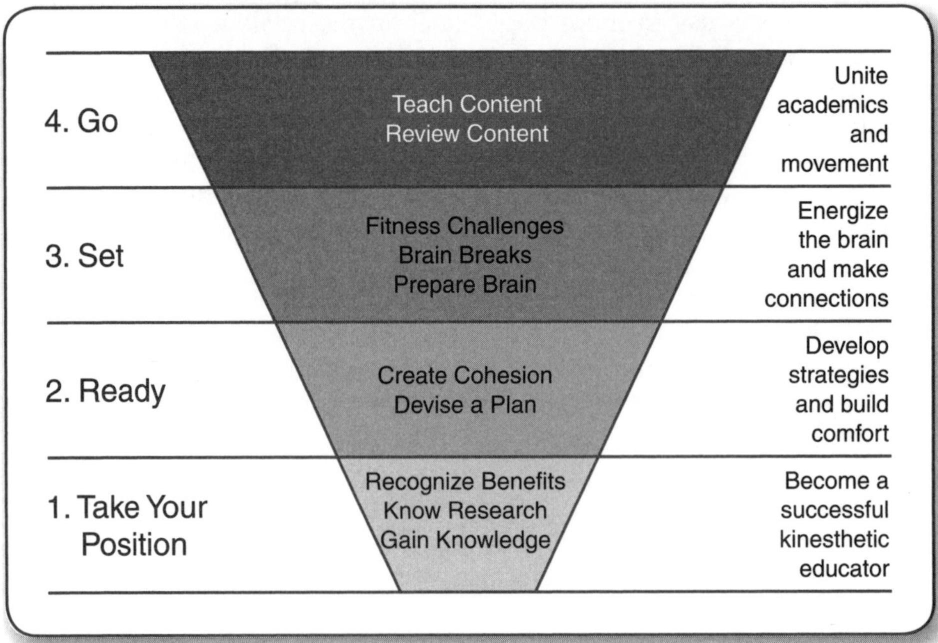

4. Go	Teach Content Review Content	Unite academics and movement
3. Set	Fitness Challenges Brain Breaks Prepare Brain	Energize the brain and make connections
2. Ready	Create Cohesion Devise a Plan	Develop strategies and build comfort
1. Take Your Position	Recognize Benefits Know Research Gain Knowledge	Become a successful kinesthetic educator

The second piece of the framework is known as "Ready." This focuses on building the classroom and/or school environment. In this portion of the framework, there is a concentration on initiating and managing a kinesthetic classroom along with creating cohesion in a vibrant setting. This aspect of the framework plays a vital role in helping you, the educator, prepare yourself, your classroom (or even your entire school), and your students for an environment that incorporates movement in both the teaching and learning process.

The third part of the framework is referred to as "Set." In this section, the emphasis is on setting your students' brain with methods, activities, and strategies that will promote optimal learning. There are three components addressed in this segment: "Preparing the Brain," "Providing Brain Breaks and Boosts," and "Supporting Exercise and Fitness." These types of movement activities take place in two minutes or less and can occur at various times in a lesson. Aside from being quick bursts of movement, they are very effective in readying the brain for enhanced learning. Moving forward, multiple activities and movements will be shared that can be incorporated into any class, including all grade levels, that will help to set the brain for peak performance.

The fourth section of the framework is titled "Go." Although this section is arguably the most desirable form of movement in a classroom environment, it's often viewed as the most challenging to implement. This area of the framework unites movement and academics while encompassing two key components: reviewing and teaching content. Using movement in the teaching and learning of academic standards is a powerful means of not only improving learning but retention as well. Teachers may find this section of the framework the most difficult because it often requires time, creativity, and out-of-the-box thinking. Throughout these upcoming chapters, teachers will receive several ideas to initiate concepts for their own classrooms and circumstances. Combining movement and academics is one of the most effective and efficient ways to enhance learning and get desired growth with indisputable results.

Part 2: Ready—Develop Strategies and Build Comfort

Build and Manage a Kinesthetic Environment

Once you have taken the position of becoming a Kinesthetic Educator, it is understandable to have concerns on how it may affect your classroom management. Let's face it; chances are most teachers have little experience moving students in a classroom environment with the goal of improving academic achievement and test scores. You may wonder if movement activities will increase discipline problems and cause a lack of control. However, once you learn to use movement purposefully, the result will more likely be an improvement in focus, productivity, and discipline. This book will spotlight what is referred to as "controlled movement with purpose." When behaviors are managed and students are learning through movement, with a distinct goal in mind, the teacher has control. In this chapter we will address motivation and hypermotivation along with effective strategies to use movement while managing various personalities and behaviors.

Create Cohesion

Is the emotional climate in your classroom vital for student learning? Absolutely! It is necessary to consider how the brain prioritizes information. The information most crucial for the brain is related to student survival needs. If these needs are not being met, then brain function is compromised, and optimal learning will be difficult. The second-most important information to the brain is that which generates emotion. What is the emotional state of your students, and can it be managed? Who is responsible for managing this state—you, your students, or perhaps a combination of both? If students are feeling stressed or uncomfortable in your classroom, it is very difficult for the brain to learn new information. The parts of the brain that use higher-level thinking strategies and critical-thinking skills shut down when an individual's mental-emotional state is compromised. The third priority of the brain is receiving data for new learning. Therefore, the emotional climate is a priority to the student's brain and plays a major role in his or her ability to learn new information (Sousa, 2017).

Part 3: Set—Make Brain Connections and Energize the Brain

Prepare the Brain

Are you familiar with the concept of whole-brain learning? Many researchers and theorists believe that specific, directed physical movements can help prepare the brain for learning while improving brain function. Although some view this research as inconclusive, others feel it is a solid combination of brain science and common sense. In this chapter we will focus on specific brain-compatible movements that improve neural connections. The ultimate goal with these movements is to improve neuron communication, so cognitive abilities can be heightened. It is believed the way we think, learn, and remember can be directly influenced by the physical movements in which we participate (Ratey, 2008). There are a number of programs that have been developed and explored to provide evidence that these movements are beneficial and effective in preparing the brain and enhancing the learning process.

Provide Brain Breaks and Boosts

Many classrooms today drive students to learn as much as they can as fast as they can. Hence, information often gets jumbled, and students are left with minimal understanding and retention. The goal of providing brain breaks and boost is to prevent academic overload while reenergizing the brain for learning. Some educators are concerned with the concept of taking a break away from academics when time already seems too short to meet all the demands of current curriculums and standards. However, if educators move quickly to "cover" the required material and learning and retention are not the result, are we really doing our students justice? It's also important to note that approximately 90 percent of the oxygen in our brain/body is stale unless we take a deep breath, yawn, or get up and move. This lack of fresh oxygen can result in confusion, lack of concentration, and memory difficulties (Blaydes Madigan, 1999). Therefore, a quick movement break can go a long way in reactivating the brain for learning.

Implement Fitness Challenges

Does supporting exercise and fitness with short stints of physical activity belong in a classroom environment? These mini challenges are a new phenomenon that is getting a lot of attention. Why? There are two main reasons. First is the thought-provoking research that shows a correlation between physical fitness and academic achievement; students who are physically fit are performing better academically. In addition, students are producing higher test scores following bouts of intense cardiorespiratory exercise. A second consideration is the serious decline in the health of our younger generation. Optimally, students would participate in physical activity in a school setting on a daily basis, preferably in physical education classes as well as outside of the school environment. However, currently, we have become a nation of "sitness" vs. fitness (Bladyes Madigan, 1999). The results are catastrophic. We are fighting a war on obesity as our youth's health deteriorates at disturbing rates. Supporting exercise and fitness in the classroom may be our best chance at putting these devastating circumstances to a halt.

Part 4: Go—Unite Academics and Movement

Review Content

Think back to any review game or activity you played as a child or adolescent. It was fun and memorable. You probably even pleaded with your teacher to play it prior to every exam. Reviewing content is a fundamental aspect of increasing retention; the more effective and perhaps enjoyable the review of the content, the greater the probability for retention. Movement is exciting and can make learning fun, engaging, and emotional. When cognitive information is linked with movement, retaining and recalling the data at a later date becomes easier (Hannaford, 1995). Memories and neural pathways fade when they are not used (Jensen, 1998). Providing multiple opportunities for review at the beginning, middle, and end of a lesson can prove invaluable. Combining this continual review of material with movement may produce even more impressive results. The movement will add a stimulating connection that heightens memory and detail. In addition, using movement to review content will awaken the brain while simultaneously providing an opportunity for it to rejuvenate. As a result, students' motivation to learn will grow as they play an active role in the learning process.

Teach Content

A true Kinesthetic Educator will eventually want to become an expert in the ability to teach academic standards through movement. Why? Learning by doing is a powerful means for understanding and retaining information. Recall something you learned by means of physically participating in the learning process, such as riding a bike. You could go years without riding a bike and still remember how to physically do it or teach it to someone else, such as a child or even a grandchild. When you experience the learning of information with your body, it's feasible that sometimes the body can remember things the brain can't. Have you ever forgotten something that you learned kinesthetically? To recall the information you may have had to physically do the movement before you could recall the data. Information and memory travel throughout the entire body, not just the brain. Therefore, it only makes sense to use both the brain and body when learning new information. Keep in mind that movement does not need to replace your usual way of teaching a concept. However, adding movement to the instruction of a concept in conjunction with other teaching methodologies can prove to have superior results, such as: increased understanding and retention, improved social skills and class cohesion, increased learner motivation, brain/body connectivity, and higher-level thinking and problem solving.

WHAT ARE THE STEPS I SHOULD TAKE TOWARD THE STARTING LINE? HOW DO I INCREASE MY SPEED?

Congratulations! You are already on your way to the starting line. If you are having any reservations of whether or not you can move students successfully in your classroom, take a deep breath and remind yourself that this can be a slow or quick process based on your comfort level. Teachers are individuals with different experiences and personalities. Your background can play a key role in dictating how quickly you grow as a Kinesthetic Educator. Your goal will be to start small and build on your use of movement in the classroom.

One of the first things we would encourage you to do is take the Kinesthetic Challenge. This involves a few small steps. Step number one is to gain as much knowledge as you can about teaching and learning through movement. During step two, share some of this information with your students while notifying them that you are going to become a Kinesthetic Educator and they will be part of a kinesthetic classroom. The third step is to implement a minimum of one quick movement activity in your classroom every day for one to three weeks. We recommend using activities from "Set" because they are less than two minutes each and are easy to implement. Once your comfort level builds, the next step is to engage your students in one review activity or teach content through movement (choosing something that is not too difficult to start off with). Finally, analyze your results. What are students saying? How are they responding to movement? Is motivation in your class growing, and are students beginning to ask for the activities? If your attitude is positive, movement will not only prove to be successful, but it will become contagious. Your students will enjoy the new direction of your classroom as they grow cognitively, physically, socially, and mentally/emotionally.

Once your challenge is complete and you recognize the benefits of being a Kinesthetic Educator, you will become more comfortable and encouraged to increase the frequency of movement in your classroom. Initially spend more time focusing on "Take your Position," "Ready," and "Set." These will be more comfortable places to begin as there is an ease of implementation, while minimal creativity is required. They also demand little planning time and can be performed in two minutes or less at any point throughout your lesson. As you engage your students in the movement activities, continue to observe their increased energy and improved learning state.

As your students' motivation grows, so will yours. Uniting movement with content is the ultimate means to increasing your speed to win the race. Although reviewing and teaching content with movement may take more planning time and creativity, you will be pleased with your efforts as your students' test scores increase, all while reaching state and national standards. You will also notice students physically moving their bodies while taking tests to help recall learned information. Instead of falling behind, students will grow with a new eagerness to learn in their interconnected classroom. In an environment filled with a variety of learners, movement is a teaching tool that will provide a multimodality approach that deserves our undivided attention.

The time to increase our speed in the educational race is today, and movement is the edge we have been searching for. Teaching and learning through movement is a universal approach that everyone can benefit from, both students and teachers alike. Ultimately, our goal in education is to provide our students with the best opportunity to become successful, productive members of society. Becoming a Kinesthetic Educator and teaching and learning through movement will allow for a comprehensive approach toward facilitating student growth and educating the whole child. This all-inclusive approach is our best chance at winning this ever-challenging race.

CHAPTER SUMMARY

- Educational Strengths: More students are graduating and seeking posteducational experiences. Students are increasing their intelligence at a younger age, and a variety of programs exist to allow learners to reach their full potential.
- Educational Weaknesses: There are physical, social, and mental/emotional concerns of our younger generation that current educational curriculums do not address or emphasize.
- The educational setting is a constant in a student's life that our society has the ability to regulate based on public needs and objectives. It is difficult to manage what happens in home environments and how children and young adults optimize their time. However, we can have direct management of what happens throughout the school day.
- To win the educational race, a sole focus on student cognition may leave us short of the finish line. A comprehensive approach that includes cognition along with the physical, social, and mental/emotional well-being of our youthful society is an all-encompassing tactic that may produce a first-place victory.
- The time to become a Kinesthetic Educator is now! You no longer have to wonder if it's in your students' best interests to incorporate movement activities into everyday teaching strategies.

> - Take Your Position: Gaining Knowledge and Developing a Philosophy of How Movement Will Best Serve Your Classroom and Students' Needs
>
> - Ready: Preparing Yourself—Building and Managing a Kinesthetic Environment and Creating Cohesion
>
> - Set: Setting Your Students' Brains—Preparing the Brain, Providing Brain Breaks and Boosts, and Supporting Exercise and Fitness
>
> - Go: Uniting Movement and Content—Reviewing Content and Teaching Content

- Teachers are individuals with different experiences and personalities. Your background can play a key role in dictating how quickly you grow as a Kinesthetic Educator. Your goal will be to start small and build on your use of movement in the classroom.
- The time to increase our speed in the educational race is today, and movement is the edge we have been searching for. Teaching and learning through movement is a universal approach that everyone can benefit from, both students and teachers alike.

TIPS FOR THE STAFF DEVELOPER

Because so many administrators and teachers are presenting on the topic of movement in the classroom, we are often asked about an outline for the presentation process. The information in this chapter is integral to that and plays an important part. A sample outline and one which you'll have to create for yourself as you move through the material in this book includes the following:

1. Understanding the brain/body connection

2. An overview of the Ready, Set, Go: Framework 2.0, including sample activities from each part of the framework

3. The nine thoughts to move by (Chapter 3)

4. Why movement enhances the teaching and learning process

5. If time allows, more activities from the framework

One more note—no matter the length of the keynote, professional development, graduate course, and so on, we never use PowerPoint! We are not against PowerPoint; it just doesn't work very well for what we do. Because of this we've made many tech support people smile!

2

Movement on the Climb

> ⇨ What continues to be the big picture in research when it comes to movement, physical activity, and physical fitness in education?
>
> ⇨ What are some examples of how teacher training and school districts have progressed over the past decade with regard to movement, physical activity, physical fitness, and overall wellness?
>
> ⇨ In regard to being physically active and creating flexible seating environments, how is the modern classroom evolving?

In taking your position to become a Kinesthetic Educator and preparing yourself to win the race and take action, it becomes important to have at least a broad-brush understanding of the research that supports this endeavor. It might also be helpful to be familiar with some of the outstanding work that is being done in schools and school districts across the nation. The idea of using movement and physical activity in the classroom has evolved, and the very best results can be seen in a three-pronged approach: (1) using movement in the classroom according to the framework that is provided herein that becomes a natural part of the school culture, (2) making aerobic activity, physical education, and physical fitness a district-wide priority, and (3) creating the modern classroom through the use of specialized furniture that allows students to be physically engaged throughout their schooling experience.

RESEARCH THAT COMPELS

In 2010 the U.S. Department of Health and Human Services Centers for Disease Control and Prevention produced a report that solidified physical activity's place in America's schools and classrooms—"The Association Between School-Based Physical Activity, Including Physical Education, and Academic Performance." The purpose of the report was to "synthesize the scientific literature that has examined the association between school-based physical activity, including physical education, and academic performance, including indicators of cognitive skills and attitudes, academic behaviors, and academic achievement" (USCDC, 2010).

This book is primarily focused on classroom physical activity. The CDC reported on nine studies that were focused specifically on classroom physical activity apart from recess or physical education. The CDC (2010) concluded: "Eight of the nine studies found positive associations between classroom-based physical activity and indicators of cognitive skills and attitudes, academic behavior, and academic achievement; none of the studies found negative associations."

The bottom line from the CDC's perspective is that there is substantial evidence that physical activity can help improve academic achievement and have an impact on cognitive skills, attitudes, and academic behavior—all components of improved academic performance. The CDC report also comments on physical education, recess, and before- and after-school extracurricular physical activity. The report can be viewed at http://www.cdc.gov/healthyschools/health_and_academics/pdf/pa-pe_paper.pdf.

This report, and many other pieces of research, compel every school and school district across the United States and around the world to answer this question: Are you interested in raising academic achievement of the students under your purview? Of course the answer is yes, which leads to an obvious follow-up question: If you haven't already, when are you going to implement regular classroom-based physical activity at all grade levels and in all content areas as a systemic approach to instruction; implement daily, quality, and fitness-oriented physical education for all students; and stop threatening recess? To be thoroughly informed, or even simply aware, of the research surrounding movement, physical activity, and physical fitness and its connection to academic achievement and to do nothing is to leave one of the most powerful tools you have at your disposal in raising the academic achievement of students on the table! You have purchased this book, so it is assumed you have some interest in the topics of the brain/body connection and movement in various forms and how they create healthier lifestyles and raise academic achievement.

The following is a four-step action plan to help get you started that will take you not more than two hours to complete:

1. Read the first two chapters of *SPARK: The Revolutionary New Science of Exercise and the Brain* (Ratey, 2008). (Please be sure and read the rest shortly thereafter.)

2. Watch Mike's TEDx Talk called "The Kinesthetic Classroom: Teaching and Learning Through Movement" (16:08), available at https://www.youtube.com/watch?v=41gtxgDfY4s.

3. Watch Paul Zientarski's TEDx Talk called "Want Smarter, Healthier Kids? Try Physical Education!" (14:11), available at https://www .youtube.com/watch?v=V81c08xyMaI.

4. Create an action plan for your classroom, building, or district! Make a call, set up a meeting, set some goals, but act!

Tony Robbins (see p. 47), international best-selling author and motivational coach to the masses says that "success leaves clues," meaning that if others are already doing something you desire to achieve, find out what and how they are doing it and copy them! Our kids' lives and academic success depend on it! Visit a school or district that is raising the health levels and academic achievement of their students because research tells us it works. There are plenty of examples available. We'll be highlighting three such school districts later in this chapter.

Some Other Research to Consider

The research supporting our creation of this framework for teachers to use movement thoughtfully and purposefully in all classrooms and content areas is quite broad. It ranges from research on how the brain prefers to learn to the cognitive and academic benefits of aerobic exercise, and from physical activity in the classroom and physical education's improving academic performance to the emotional environment that is so critical to classroom success. It's been almost two decades since a 2002 California study showed the relationship between higher FitnessGram scores and higher standard achievement test scores. These results have been replicated in other studies numerous times. John Ratey's landmark bestseller *SPARK: The Revolutionary Science of Exercise and the Brain* (mentioned previously in this chapter), which highlighted exactly what aerobic exercise does for academic performance and cognitive function, was first released almost a decade ago. By the way, if you don't own or haven't read this book and are a parent, teacher, administrator, or just someone who cares about your own brain health, you need to stop what you are doing, go to your computer, and order your copy. It's that important. The research and discussion in *SPARK* go far beyond the walls of a school building to topics such as stress, depression, attention deficient hyperactivity disorder (ADHD), addiction, and aging.

Our original book *The Kinesthetic Classroom: Teaching and Learning Through Movement* was published in January of 2010, which means we had been reading research and creating activities in 2008 and 2009. What has happened since then in this growing and robust field of research? How far have we come in our understanding of how movement, physical activity, physical fitness, and aerobic activity enhance student learning and improve academic achievement? Here are highlights of some of the latest findings:

- Research from the University of Kansas showed data that support the link between physical activity, cognitive function, and academic achievement and that physically active academic lessons of moderate intensity improved overall performance on a standardized test of academic achievement by 6 percent compared to a decrease of 1 percent for controls (Donnelly & Lambourne, 2011).
- Research from the University of Southern Mississippi showed a statistically significant positive correlation between fitness and standardized test scores in language arts and math and a statistically significant negative relationship with absences (Blom, Alvarez, Zhang, & Kolbo, 2011).
- Research conducted in the Charlotte-Mecklenburg Schools showed that students in Grades 3 to 6 who met the Charlotte-Mecklenburg Schools fitness standards also showed significant growth in reading and math (Wooten Green, 2016).
- Excessive sitting is associated with heart disease and type 2 diabetes even if a person is meeting the American Heart Association recommendation of at least 150 minutes of moderate intensity exercise a week (Owen, Healy, Matthews, & Dunstan, 2010).
- A review of research published in the *British Medical Journal* concluded that even short bursts of exercise—10 to 40 minutes—lead to an immediate boost in concentration (Konigs, Oosterlaan, Scherder, & Verbeurgh, 2014).
- Researchers at the Wake Forest School of Medicine found that adults with mild cognitive impairment who exercised over a six-month period experienced greater gains in brain volume than those who just stretched (Radiological Society of North America, 2016).
- A recent study examined the physical activity of 153 Finnish children between the ages of six and eight. Activity was measured through heart rate monitors and movement sensors. Academic skills were evaluated through standardized school tests. The boys who spent the most time sitting and least amount of time moving had poorer reading skills than the rest of the group. This was also found in the math skills of the youngest boys (Brage et al., 2016).

- Findings published in *Preventive Medicine* reviewed studies involving more than 1 million people and concluded that moderately strenuous aerobic exercise had a large and significant effect against depression (Firth et al., 2016).

These represent just some of the latest findings that echo earlier research that will lead to an even greater understanding of how movement, physical activity, aerobic activity, and physical fitness enhance cognitive function and academic achievement.

ENTRY POINT: THE KINESTHETIC CLASSROOM

In 2008, the two of us did something somewhat radical in the educational world. We produced a graduate course on movement and physical activity in the classroom—The Kinesthetic Classroom: Teaching and Learning Through Movement. Eight years after the first course was field-tested, more than 4,400 teachers in the states of Pennsylvania, Maryland, and New Jersey had completed the course. Offered by the Regional Training Center in partnership with La Salle University and the College of New Jersey, the next step will be to offer it online to reach even more teachers, which will have happened by the printing of this book. For more information on this course and program, visit www.thertc.net.

The course stemmed from a natural partnership between the two of us. Traci is a public school health and physical education teacher and graduate instructor for the Regional Training Center. Mike, now academic director for the Regional Training Center, was mostly teaching graduate courses on the brain and multiple intelligences. Influenced by Howard Gardner and Eric Jensen, we were both using extensive movement activities with adult learners as brain breaks and ways to teach content, even though it wasn't written into the curriculum. What we were finding was that participants were commenting on their final projects about how movement and physical activity were changing their classrooms for the better—sometimes more so than the many concepts and principles built into the curriculum. It motivated us to dig into the research and design a curriculum and framework for teachers to use movement and physical activity thoughtfully and purposefully in all learning contexts, no matter the grade level or content area. It was an instant hit.

Today, The Kinesthetic Classroom: Teaching and Learning Through Movement sits comfortably in the M.Ed. programs of both La Salle University and the College of New Jersey. It is a highly rated and well-received course. How many M.Ed. programs have courses that deal only with movement, physical activity, and physical fitness in their curricula? In 2013, The Kinesthetic Classroom II: Moving Through the Curriculum was designed, field-tested, and offered to teachers in the same three states. It's having similar success as the original.

Although they are still in the minority, more and more colleges and universities are offering classes to their undergrad and graduate students on the benefits of using movement and physical activity in classrooms. In fact, the University of Mississippi now offers a bachelor of arts in education with a 12-hour wellness and physical activity endorsement. The slogan for this forward-thinking program is "Integrate wellness and physical activity, activate the brain and body, educate the whole child." It is programs like these, specifically designed for undergraduates, that have the potential to change the face of education. For more information on this University of Mississippi program, go to www.teachwell.olemiss.edu.

THREE SCHOOL-BASED EDUCATIONAL SUCCESS STORIES

THE ALIEF SCHOOL DISTRICT, HOUSTON TX

Contributed by Kelley Sullivan, Alief ISD Wellness Coordinator

(Author's Note: Jean Blaydes Moize, who wrote the foreword for The Kinesthetic Classroom: Teaching and Learning Through Movement, is the creator of Action-Based Learning. The terms and meaning behind "action-based learning" and "kinesthetic classroom" are considerably aligned in the movement-based approach to teaching they promote.)

I have always been a believer in the connection between movement and learning. Having seen Jean Blaydes Moize more than a decade ago prompted me to have her train our physical education teachers and some classroom teachers in the connections among movement, learning, and the brain. For those of us in physical education, the concept that movement helped with behavior and learning was an easy sell. In that first training, it became evident that classroom teachers could also be persuaded. Every classroom teacher lucky enough to attend the training became a believer that this is what was best for kids.

One of my early in-district collaborators, Laura Klubert, was trained by Eric Jensen, and she too understood the relationship between physical activity and learning. For years, we preached to teachers and administrators about the value and benefit of movement. At that time, however, it was just that—preaching and stating our beliefs—we did not have the data behind our words to support the idea.

In 2001, I moved from being a physical education teacher to a classroom teacher, teaching reading to students in ninth grade who were not reading on grade level. During my second year of teaching this class, the school started some morning clubs to keep students occupied before the school day started. I noticed that those students who attended the cardio and basketball clubs came to first period much more awake and focused. My belief in action-based learning soared.

When our new superintendent came on board in 2011, it became clear that he too believed that getting kids up and moving was important. New data was available, and at the first meeting he had with district administrators, he shared the

John Medina video clip about Brain Rule #1—Exercise Boosts Brain Power (see at https://www.youtube.com/watch?v=ck-tQtOSOOs). It was the same message that Laura and I had been offering for years, but coming from the superintendent created a significant difference for campus administrators. Buy-in was increasing, so we began gathering all the research available to us to sell action-based learning as a viable academic option for Alief campuses.

During the 2013–2014 school year, Laura and I began visiting the few campuses in the Houston area that had action-based learning labs and looked at their data. In April of the same year, we gave a short 45-minute presentation to principals and administrators about the concept of action-based learning and the incorporation of action-based learning labs.

We shared data from other campuses in South Carolina and Pasadena (Texas) ISD as well. Before the presentation was even finished, we had text messages from principals saying they were in and wanted this program for their campus. Because administrative support is key in successful implementation, this was a major accomplishment.

Laura and I put in a request for the following year to add a few action-based learning labs on select campuses as pilot programs. To our surprise, the answer was yes. Administration wanted us to be prepared for the labs to be ready by September of the following year. This was great news, but the time frame was short. We had to come up with a framework for implementation and training, choose the campuses, and work out the logistics of location and oversight. We decided on four campuses where principals had already shown interest and who had a location for a lab. The only exception was Best Elementary. At the time, Best Elementary was our lowest-performing school; improvement was required according to the Texas Education Agency (TEA). They were hiring a new principal who was not yet on board and were submitting a turnaround plan to the state. Labs were put on this campus to be used as part of their TEA plan. The plan included hiring someone who had buy-in for action-based learning, but when Renee Canales was hired, she was not familiar with the concept! Renee agreed to attend Action Based Learning Certification training in South Carolina (now called Action Based Learning/Kinesthetic Classroom Certification Training). That was a major turning point for action-based learning in our district and especially at Best Elementary.

All of this happened during the summer of 2014. By the start of the 2014–2015 school year, labs were set up at six campuses. We had facilitators at each campus and met with them regularly to get this off the ground in a successful way. We sent each facilitator to a certified training and worked with them to train teachers on how to use the labs. At the same time this was happening, our teacher induction program was adding required trainings for all new teachers in Alief. As part of our induction program, any new teacher is required to have 35 hours of prescriptive professional development for district priority programs. Because of the good feedback we were receiving about movement and learning and behavior, the district approached me and asked if we would provide seven hours of training in action-based learning to make sure that teachers had the knowledge and tools necessary to incorporate movement into their everyday teaching. This training was not necessarily about the labs but in helping teachers to understand the benefits of movement in the teaching and learning process. This training provided a real turning point in movement and learning taking off in Alief. Teachers began implementing this concept as part of best practices. Movement in the classroom was becoming more the normal way of doing things.

Since the original labs were installed, we have added labs at eight more campuses. Alief now has 14 campuses with full labs, five high schools with some kinesthetic furniture in structured classrooms, and many more campuses that have added a variety of seating options for students. Most elementary campuses have morning movement to start the day; at one time that was all we had for movement and learning. However, teachers and principals now understand that movement should be included throughout the school day, not just in the morning. Campus support has been a large part of the success of the program. Once individual campuses started talking about their great success with behavior and academic focus, more campuses have added labs and kinesthetic classroom equipment. We teach that action-based learning is not a program and not a lab but a concept of teaching that should be incorporated throughout the school day. We train our physical education teachers to add academic concepts to movement and train our classroom teachers to add movement to the academics they already teach. We envision that all Alief campuses have some sort of action-based learning going on, and we have seen evidence of it in classroom walkthrough visits.

Figure 2.1   Second Grade Math and Reading Comparison Data

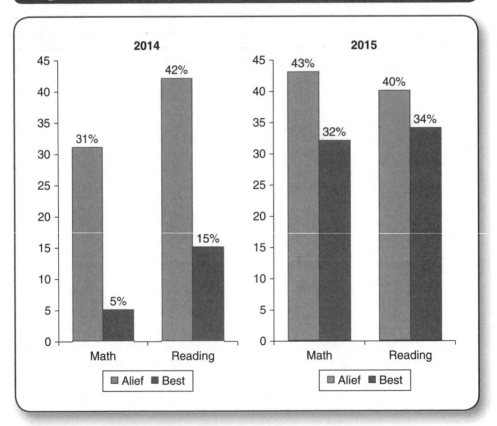

Source: Courtesy of Best Elementary, Alief Independent School District.

Figure 2.2   Texas Education Agency Performance Index Report Data Comparison

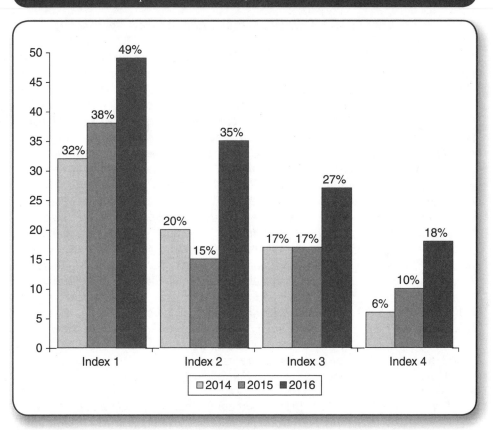

Source: Courtesy of Best Elementary, Alief Independent School District.

Our anecdotal data is very clear and positive—teachers overall say this has reduced behavior issues and increased focus across the board. At one of our alternative high schools, behavior referrals were reduced by more than 50 percent! At one elementary campus, a pilot intervention program was implemented for math and reading using an action-based learning lab for some students and traditional intervention for others. One hundred percent of students in the pilot action-based program passed the state test in comparison with 33 percent of those in the regular intervention. Data from Best Elementary showed tremendous improvement after the implementation of action-based learning in classrooms, installation of an action-based learning lab, and aerobic, or kinesthetic, classroom equipment in some classrooms.(See Figures 2.1 and 2.2).

The trio of implementing action-based learning in classrooms, adding action-based learning labs on many of our campuses, and installing kinesthetic classroom equipment in many classrooms has dramatically added to the academic success of the student population in Alief.

THE POTTSTOWN SCHOOL DISTRICT, POTTSTOWN, PA

Contributed by David Genova, Pottstown School District Wellness Coordinator

Pottstown School District (PSD) is one of 28 urban school districts in the Commonwealth of Pennsylvania, with an enrollment of 3,061 students. It is the poorest school district in one of the richest counties in the state. Located in Western Montgomery County, Pottstown is a community of high poverty with many of the accompanying social problems, where the borough of Pottstown and school district are contiguous within a 5.5-square-mile area. Pottstown serves as the hub for social services in western Montgomery County, bringing many at-risk families to the area in search of services. The community of Pottstown has a per capita income of $20,923, where 31 percent of residents earn less than $25,000 and 53.4 percent of the population is minority. Almost half of Pottstown's children under the age of 18 are in households headed by a one parent figure. Because of the large number of students from low-income families, 100 percent of students receive free/reduced lunch, which is considerably higher than Pennsylvania's average of 34.3 percent. PSD supports a 20 percent special needs population with students who have intellectual disabilities, autism, and social emotional problems. The district supports its own life skills classes and autism programs. The population is ethnically diverse with 33 percent African American, 13 percent Hispanic, 42 percent Caucasian, and 10 percent multiracial. I felt it was important to provide this context when examining the success we've had in implementing physical, activity-based, and other types of wellness programs.

As a district it is important to note the following:

- *It is policy of the PSD that we are committed to provide a school environment that promotes and protects children's health, well-being, and ability to learn by supporting physical activity.*
- *Students K–12 have the opportunity, support, and encouragement to be physically active on a regular basis.*
- *Our schools provide physical education to foster lifelong habits of physical activity and establish links between health education and school meal programs so that students will be prepared to make healthy choices.*
- *School administrators establish, coordinate, and monitor physical activity policy as it relates to their buildings.*

Morning exercise, before-, during-, and after-school physical activity programs, action-based learning, and flexible seating are some of the ways students of the PSD are physically active. The district is working collectively to reach the common goal of helping students excel in the classroom. "Action-based learning supports everything we know is good for kids," says Matthew Moyer, Rupert Elementary School principal. "It engages our students' bodies and their minds in their learning and increases student engagement." PSD understands that learning and health are related. In fact they are interrelated. The planning of our programs relies extensively on the School Health Index report that was used to assess the strengths and weaknesses of PSD's wellness strategy. PSD is moving toward the comprehensive Whole School, Whole Community, Whole Child model. The vision focuses not only on physical education and nutrition but also on social and emotional climate, the physical environment, family engagement, and community involvement.

We have embraced the need for a culture of wellness and have started moving forward on a number of physical and mental wellness initiatives. If wellness is important to our superintendent, it must be important to the principals; if it's important to the principals, it must be important to the teachers; and if it's important to the teachers, it must be important to students. PSD recognizes the significant impact that efficient and sustainable school health teams can have on building successful school wellness programs. School health teams come in a variety of shapes and sizes, but they always have a common goal: to rally forces to make schools healthier. Together, wellness teams build champions to identify health concerns, lead projects that promote health, raise funds, promote and celebrate successful health initiatives, and develop resources to help others replicate their efforts.

PSD has wellness teams in each of the six schools. They have been created to enhance the acceptance and success of the wellness program activities by encouraging staff and student's ownership of the program. They are the arms, legs, eyes, and ears of the program, providing valuable insight to the district wellness coordinator. Team members are responsible to assist with program planning and actively promote program activities among coworkers and students. They provide thoughts, ideas, and suggestions from their coworkers and students. Team members communicate to the wellness coordinator what other employees and students are thinking, feeling, and saying. They communicate to their coworkers what the nutrition and physical activity program is all about and why they should be involved. They help with staff wellness events, distribute materials, collect participant tracking forms, and speak to other staff/student groups.

Over the last three years PSD has participated in the Boeing Center for Children's Wellness School Wellness Checklist Contest. In 2014–2015 PSD was one of the seven public school districts in the Pottstown area offered the opportunity to participate in a pilot replication of a school-based obesity prevent model, Docs Adopt School Health Initiative (DASHI). PSD applied and was chosen to be part of the pilot by the Pottstown Area Health and Wellness Foundation, who funded the project. PSD applied and was chosen again in 2015–2016 to participate in an expanded DASHI pilot that includes 21 schools. PSD accounts for 29 percent of all the pilot schools, with 100 percent of the elementary schools participating. Franklin Elementary earned $3,000 and was named the Boeing Center for Children's Wellness Achievement Award Champion for implementing the highest number of proven wellness strategies among the participating schools. Examples include having a school wellness team, incorporating physical activity in the classrooms, participating in safe routes to school, offering yoga to students, promoting physical activity in after-school programs, and offering healthy cooking classes.

The wellness coordinator continues to monitor the success of school wellness initiatives daily, including levels of participation, quality of activities, and impact on participants. Each week the wellness coordinator monitors each building's initiatives and activities. The wellness coordinator meets with the superintendent, supervisor of curriculum, and wellness committees monthly to provide updates and address issues. In addition the wellness coordinator reviews the program budget with the business office. Our superintendent created a brain energizer committee team of school building administrators, classroom teachers, physical education teachers, nurses, therapists, and psychologists. This committee meets quarterly to address each building's wellness strategies, goals, and outcomes. By doing this, our superintendent is holding every building accountable.

An important component of building capacity is engaging the families and local community in whole child wellness efforts. Currently, we have a family advisory committee (FAC) comprised of community leaders who initiate change in the community. The FAC was started by Pottstown Early Action for Kindergarten Readiness (PEAK) Coordinator Mary Reick and in partnership with the W. K. Kellogg Foundation. The FAC facilitates community conversations in which they discuss key issues in education with local families to develop a network of neighborhood support. Moving forward, the FAC will focus community conversations around health and wellness. This aligns with the focus priority of Pottstown's organization of faith-based institutions, Project Inspiration. The religious leaders in the area have identified health and wellness as a priority area of need for our population. A wellness focus for the FAC would be well supported in our community.

Family and community involvement in school-based physical activity provides numerous benefits. Research shows that youth participation in physical activity is influenced by participation and support of parents and siblings. When families are active together, they spend additional time together and experience health benefits. Families can support a comprehensive school physical activity program by participating in evening/weekend special events and parents/guardians serving as activity volunteers. Through community engagement, we work with the Pottstown community (key leaders from faith, business, education, and government organizations) to get input and to build support for the family engagement process. Community involvement allows maximum use of school and community resources (e.g., facilities and personnel) and creates a connection between school- and community-based physical activity opportunities. Joint-use agreements or partnerships are an example of formal school-community collaboration. When the district promotes the health and well-being of students, staff, classrooms, and schools, we are developing an environment that is most conducive to effective teaching and learning. When we learn who our students are, enhancing connectedness between them and the school, we not only increase their sense of belonging and safety, but we also better understand what makes our students tick and can better adjust learning methodologies. When we reach out to families and the local community, we not only expand the safety net, but we also empower key stakeholders in the responsibility and purpose of education. Partnerships between PSD and community organizations are imperative for the success and sustainability of our school wellness programs. Key partnerships help to create support that enables children and youth to learn and succeed and help families and communities thrive. Our partnerships bring together diverse individuals and groups to expand opportunities for children, families, and the community.

Over the last three years, PSD administration took district employees to the Pottstown Area Health and Wellness Foundation Annual Conference called Healthy Bodies Healthy Mind Institute. Leading neuroscientists, educators, and psychologists share best practices and evidence-based research to creatively incorporate physical activity into teaching practices and enhance students' ability to learn. This conference also gives the building wellness teams an opportunity to action plan and create annual goals by sharing thoughts, ideas, and suggestions. As you can see by the district's attendance numbers, school wellness has become a priority to everyone. In 2013, 43 staff members attended, in 2014,

61 staff members, and in 2015, 74 staff members. These numbers include new and returning team members, including administrators and school board members. Staff returned to the district energized with exciting information and ideas to activate student learning potential. A brain energizer committee, including administrators, principals, nurses, and teachers, were formed after attending the summer institute. The gathering of this committee provides a chance to discuss the current challenges, benefits, and district goals that schools are experiencing in regard to school wellness.

It is critical for teachers to have ongoing and regular opportunities to learn from each other. PSD provides ongoing professional development that keeps teachers up to date on new health-related research on how children learn, tools for the classroom, and how to incorporate physical activity into the classroom and curriculum. The best professional development is ongoing, experiential, collaborative, connected to, and derived from working with students and understanding their culture. Continued efforts to identify funding sources and practice sound fiscal management and resource allocation are critical district activities and have full institutional support. The school district will continue to identify potential funding sources and develop and submit grant applications in support of our wellness mission.

In 2014 the district was awarded a grant, half of which was used to encourage children to be active during class time. These funds were used to purchase kinesthetic desks through a company called Kidsfit. Desks purchased through the grant have pedals where students can ride it like a bike, whereas others resemble a strider exercise machine. Our high school's special education classroom converted a traditional classroom into a kinesthetic classroom. We removed their traditional desks and chairs and replaced them with seven simple movement desks that 12 students can use at one time. These motion desks and tables allow children to be in motion while they learn. We have a variety of desks that include pedal desks, strider desks, and ellipse desks. We also have four kinesthetic desks in one classroom at Rupert Elementary where a fourth-grade teacher reported that students have fewer disciplinary problems when they use the kinesthetic desks and the exercise equipment in the classroom. "They are more engaged in what they are learning because, as they are actively working out their brains, they are actively listening," she said. Data collected on students using the kinesthetic desks showed a significant decrease in behavioral issues.

As a district we noticed in classrooms that teachers were allowing their students to stand next to their desks. Although students were standing, they still had to bend over to use their desks. Providing classrooms with elevated desks would help students be focused and keep them be more comfortable at the same time. From a grant, $2,000 was given to the Pottstown High School construction technology program to purchase materials to make standing desks. A group of 15 high school students built the desks. Some of the seniors actually helped design the desks as well as construct them. Construction Technology Instructor Kyle O'Neill said two different standing desks are used throughout the district. The elementary schools have bigger full-desk stations that multiple children can surround. At the high school, the standing desks are built more like podiums. We currently have 36 standing desks in the district: 21 in the elementary schools, six in the middle school, and nine in the high school. Because not every student is equipped with a standing desk, teachers have implemented standing desk stations in the classroom and created a rotation schedule for their use. This allows freedom to move and relax instead of concentrating specifically on sitting still, in addition to whatever concept is being outlined by the teacher.

PSD is a walking school district, where the majority of students walk to school each day. The "walking school bus" is a fun and healthy way for kids (and volunteers from the community) to get regular exercise and prepare themselves for a day of learning. The walking school bus is a group of students accompanied by adult volunteers who walk an assigned route every day with "stops" along the way to pick up children and then complete the walk to the elementary school. With more than one-third of Pottstown students now obese or overweight, it is more important than ever to model a healthy, active lifestyle.

Currently, we run a walking school bus for the attendance area of one of our four elementary schools. This program requires a large commitment and collaboration from PSD employees and the community. Many of our walking volunteers are employees of area businesses or part of Pottstown community organizations. About 80 percent of the 40 volunteers represent local businesses. The walking school bus was created as a healthy and safe form of transportation for students. Many parents have been asking for a solution to the school district's nonbusing policy, which is how the walking school bus program began. The University of Sciences in Philadelphia is partnering with the school district on the walking school bus program to do a case study. The purpose of this study is to see how the implementation of a walking school bus program at Rupert Elementary school impacts students in the following areas: student attendance, student arrival time to school, student physical activity level, student's body mass index, student academic success, and changes in student behavior.

According to PedNet, most walking school buses around the United States operate at most once per week. Rupert Elementary School operates their walking school bus five days per week all school year long. We do this for two reasons; (1) equity and (2) to meet transportation needs. Rupert Elementary School's walking school bus offers three color-coded routes (pink, orange, and yellow). The pink route is the longest (1.66 miles) and in the 2015–2016 school year averaged 20 children. In the current school year (2016–2017), the pink route has almost doubled, averaging 38 children. The orange route (0.92 miles) averages 10 children, whereas the yellow route (1.42 miles) averages three children. Our program offers walk-stops as well as door-to-door services. Our predetermined walk-stops are no more than two blocks from a child's home. Our 40 or so volunteers pick these children up every day along their route at designated stops and designated times. The routes were determined based on where the majority of our children live. We wanted to make sure we were going to reach as many children as possible.

Finally, Pottstown also offers its students the following programs, "Girls on the Run," a 12-week program that operates in the spring; "ABC's of Fitness," an after-school physical activity program; "AM Exercise," a before-school physical activity program for fifth- and sixth-grade students; and "The Walking Classroom," a program used by two fifth-grade classrooms that allows for walking around a track three times a week while listening to an academic lesson on a podcast.

With a firm understanding of how wellness and physical activity influence learning and academic achievement, PSD will continue to support and grow these initiatives to better the schooling experience for the whole child and all Pottstown students.

THE EMERGENCE OF ACTION-BASED LEARNING LABS

Contributed by Cindy Hess and Jean Blaydes Moize

Cindy Hess

During my normal summer reading research, one article in particular caught my attention. A special education professor, Dr. Lyle Palmer of Wynona University in Minnesota, discussed his stimulating maturity through accelerated readiness training (SMART) program. This became my inspiration to teach differently! I had recently been moved to the lowest-performing school in our district and began applying the SMART concept to my instruction, especially at the first- and second-grade level. I observed that not only were the students performing better in physical education class, but they also seemed easier to manage.

During the following summer I continued to read and reread current brain research and decided to approach my principal. Because we were the lowest-performing elementary building in our district, I knew just how to phrase my approach. Our kindergarten children had no physical education—none! My goal was simply to get the kindergarten children in physical education with no expectations of anything else. Simply put, I was looking for a back-door method to get those kids. I made an appointment with my principal during the summer of 2000, and here was my opening statement: I can help you improve the reading scores of our students! When she stopped laughing, I laid out my plan! I would take the kindergarten kids straight off the bus first thing in the morning during the 20-minute unpacking, getting ready prior to announcements time. It was basically preparation time for me and noninstructional time for the kids!

I explained about Dr. Palmer's work, and we decided to stay with the SMART program name. Dr. Palmer used and studied five basic movement stations in his program: crawling, rolling, spinning, tracing, and tracking. I would start two weeks into the school year, so students would know where their classroom was and the initial adjustment to being in school would be over. The kindergarten teachers were skeptical at best! At that time we had half-day kindergarten, so I used 20 minutes of lunch to run the program for the afternoon kindergarten classes. I was armed with research to justify the program but had absolutely no idea what I was doing, yet I succeeded. I saw kindergartners every morning for approximately 15 minutes of purposeful activity. The first three weeks exceeded my expectations. After two weeks the kindergarten teachers stormed my gym demanding to know what I was doing! They had changed their entire morning due to the fact that the kids were ready to go; there was no more weather and no more calendars to start the morning. They jumped right into the meat of the lesson.

I was also noticing that the children had mastered the stations. Nothing in my research showed this. Then the lightbulb went off! Dr. Palmer did all his research on special needs and low-functioning students. I needed to begin developing and creating new stations and progressions to challenge my students. Thankfully I had been well educated on developmental physical education and had a ready source of research to build on. Just as I was ready to change the stations and move to the next progression, my principal announced that the lab was being shut down. The curriculum coordinator heard all the talk within the staff and decided that it was not fair for only one school to have this program. I was determined not to give this up, so I proposed we run the program for one year as a pilot. We would collect data using the "dibbles test" and compare our kindergarten scores to the other buildings. It worked! We were back in action a week later, and the year was a success.

As the kids progressed I created the next developmental appropriate station and still had no idea what I was doing. I knew the program was successful in getting kindergarten students daily physical education, but I had no idea the impact the program was making on behavior and achievement. At the end of the school year, we gathered as a team to look at data. Our building had moved to the highest-scoring kindergarten, and the teachers shared all the benefits they had observed over the school year. The growth was observed in every aspect of development— they followed directions better, showed better scissors skills, and had better transitions between learning centers, lining up, and so on. The kindergarten teachers raved so much that the first-grade teachers wanted in on SMART.

The district office noticed as well. The decision was made to send my principal and me to Minnesota for training at A Chance to Grow, where I had the pleasure of meeting Dr. Palmer. It was also decided that all kindergartens would begin receiving SMART, and our first grade would continue the study. The training, further research, and making connections began to give me the understanding I needed about why this was working and how to make the program better. I kicked off 2001 with K–1 daily physical education using the SMART program and added second grade the following year. In the winter of 2002 I met Jean Blaydes at a workshop held at Millersville University sponsored by our Lancaster/Lebanon chapter of the American Alliance for Health, Physical Education, Recreation and Dance (AAHPERD), now SHAPE—Society for Health and Physical Educators. I felt a connection to her presentation and worked with my administration to bring her to my school district the following school year for staff development. After this staff development in 2003, Jean and I decided we were the other half of each other's brains. With a handshake, we began our journey. Together we prepared to launch the SMART KIDS program at the Leaning and the Brain Expo in Orlando, Florida, the summer of 2004. After this conference, to protect the program, the HIGHLAND SMART program became the Action-Based Learning Lab.

Data From the SMART Program at Highland Elementary School

Kindergarten Letter Identification

2000–2001—May: 73%
2001–2002—May: 72%
2002–2003—May: 96%

Grade 1 Letter Identification

2000–2001
    September: 33%
    May: 96%
2001–02
    September: 57%
    May: 96%
2002–2003
    September: 70%
    May: 100%

The yearly increase in September retention rates was due to the fact that I got better at reinforcing academics each year. When I introduced the learning ladder during the second year of the program, the retention rates soared! As shown the retention rate from kindergarteners tested in September of first grade increased each year—33 percent (this group did not have the ladder station) 57 percent, and 70 percent. Retention is critical as it cuts down on reteaching time! At the end of the third year, when second grade was also included in the program, we had only four of 220 kindergarteners through second graders not reading on grade level. It was amazing—the lowest-performing school moved to being the highest! It was a gratifying transformation that in part led to the emergence of the Action-Based Learning Lab.

Jean Blaydes Moize

Action-based learning concepts are based on brain research that supports the link of movement to learning. The programs and strategies used in action-based learning are designed to teach academics kinesthetically to improve academic performance, behavior, and wellness. Action-based learning has two parts: one tangible and one intangible. The intangible part of action-based learning is the philosophy that intentional movement enhances learning and that kinesthetic teaching strategies increase memory retention and retrieval. Teachers who have a general knowledge of how the brain learns can use action-based learning, brain-compatible lessons that help all students learn better. My book Thinking on Your Feet *has more than 200 lessons that put kinesthetic learning into action.*

The tangible parts of action-based learning are the action-based learning labs and the kinesthetic classroom furniture by Kidsfit. The labs are designed to benefit all students using age-appropriate, brain-based activities to fill in developmental gaps and prepare the brain for learning. What sets the action-based learning labs apart is that students are reinforcing and reviewing academic concepts while they are performing physical tasks. Brain research suggests that when physical tasks are combined with cognitive tasks, the brain increases focus and attention. Action-based learning labs include the Primary Lab for Grades PreK–2, the Body Brain Adventure Lab for Grades 3–6, and the NeuroNasium Lab for secondary students Grades 6–12.

My philosophy is that every child can learn and that every child's level of health and wellness can improve. My mission and goal is to change the world one little heart and one little brain at a time. That passion drives me to spread the message of action-based learning everywhere. With the success of action-based learning concepts building in classrooms and gymnasiums, I knew there had to be a way to put the brain science, child development concepts, and physical education practices together to create brain-based, brain-compatible, kid-friendly, and teacher-friendly programs to help increase the health and learning of all students.

I began to create stations based on what I had learned from Jack Capon's Perceptual-Motor Learning. Stations seemed to be a successful way to manage large numbers of primary students. In 2002 I presented in Pennsylvania, where I met an exceptional physical educator, Cindy Hess. Her district invited me to present in 2003. Cindy shared her program called the SMART Lab with me. I was shocked to discover that we were thinking exactly alike! It was like she was the other half of my brain and vice versa! Cindy's program had already impacted her students, school, and district with great results. We decided to join forces to start sharing and selling the action-based learning labs. We then developed what became the Body Brain Adventure Lab and NeuroNasium Lab to provide labs for all grade levels.

For her SMART program, Cindy had designed a learning ladder for Station 6 progressions. For my version, I had designed the ABC Pathways Mat for Station 4 progressions. We combined both into our lab. These two unique pieces of equipment set us apart from other motor labs. Both are patented and have since become recognizable symbols of the Action-Based Learning Lab. In the beginning, our learning ladders were made by an Amish man named Abram, who lived close to Cindy in Pennsylvania. He made each ladder by hand with no electricity. Later when Abram was unable to make the ladders, Kidsfit in Huger, South Carolina, took over production. That was the beginning of my relationship with Ed Pinney and his family at Kidsfit.

Kidsfit shares my philosophy and vision to spread the message of action-based learning. Ed has designed unique, innovative equipment for our labs. He is masterful in making ideas come to life. Kidsfit also manufactures kinesthetic desks and tables for the classroom so that every student can move to learn. Kidsfit products are now sold internationally and have won awards for design and quality. One award described the Kidsfit kinesthetic furniture as the "Classroom of the Future." In 2016, Action-Based Learning joined forces with Kidsfit to further establish action-based learning into the future of education. I consider it a "God Thing" and a blessing in my life.

The research and data from action-based learning labs nationwide has shown increased student performance, improved behavior, and decreased absenteeism. A research study conducted by pediatricians at the Medical University of South Carolina showed that students using action-based learning programs improved in three areas necessary for learning. Their research results were cited as one of 14 studies that supported the need for intentional movement in learning. Although so many other schools have positive data using the labs, Crossroads High School in Houston, Texas, is one school with exceptional results. Crossroads is designed for at-risk students who are behind in academic credits and are at risk of not graduating from high school. Students there visited the NeuroNasium for 30 minutes per day for four days per week on average. Classroom teachers implemented action-based learning strategies to teach academics kinesthetically. In one year, there was a 78 percent higher passing rate for the four core subjects. The more hours spent in the NeuroNasium, the higher the grade point average for each student. There were also 63 percent less behavior referrals.

THE EVOLVING CLASSROOM OF THE 21ST CENTURY

In February of 2013, Nilofer Merchant gave a TED Talk (see https://www.ted.com/talks/nilofer_merchant_got_a_meeting_take_a_walk) where she coined the phrase "sitting is the smoking of our generation"—that we sit (9.5 hours a day) more than we sleep (7.7 hours)—in a brief presentation about walking meetings. That six-word bombshell has become the unofficial slogan of a paradigm shift from sitting as the norm and standing as "taking a break" to standing as the norm and sitting to take a break.

In another must-see TED Ed animation "Why Sitting Is Bad for You" (see https://www.youtube.com/watch?v=wUE18KrMz14), Murat Dalkilinc describes the hazards of sitting—from agitating our bodies and overworking the muscles around our spine to being linked to several types of cancer and heart disease. The bottom line is that our bodies are built to move, and our brains work better when doing so. Extended periods of sitting are exactly what most students at all levels of education and training are exposed to. Entering most American classrooms in 2017 could well evoke images of what a child might have experienced 100 years ago or more—save the technology, of course. Static desks and chairs still dominate the landscape. Unfortunately, this has been the norm for hundreds of years, but times are changing and changing at a rate that will transform classrooms around the world over the coming decades. What exactly is changing? There is a relatively new focus on movement and physical activity in the classroom combined with engineering and manufacturing wizardry. It's upping the game and changing how children experience the modern classroom and learning.

EDUCATIONAL INCARCERATION

Contributed by Dave Spurlock, Retired Physical Educator, Charleston County School District

I was a public school teacher for 33 years, and I mandated classroom behavior to follow rules that I had learned in college classroom management 101. Twenty-five students sat in 25 desks, each with his or her feet flat on the floor and hands on the desktop where they could be seen at all times. They would be sentenced to their 2'x2' cell for eight hours a day. Some would call this "educational incarceration." As I understand incarceration, even prisoners are allowed "yard time." This is how we have taught our children for generations. How has that worked out so far? Could we change that paradigm to something that would actually benefit students? Could we develop a strategy and alter the mind-set of our educational practices that would benefit our student brains, behaviors, and bodies?

After my 33 years of teaching, I became the Charleston County School District physical education coordinator. I knew that it was my task to make physical education an important component of each school's curriculum. It helped that the state of South Carolina had just passed new legislation to increase funding for physical education. The legislation also increased the number of minutes schools were required to provide physical education and physical activity. This was to counteract No Child Left Behind—which set math and English as the most important components of education. Educators and administration would be evaluated on that criteria, not on physical education.

I was looking for a reason that would keep physical education, teachers, and classes in our school day. I heard about a school in Naperville, Illinois, that had taken kids who were having learning difficulties in English and were put into physical education classes immediately before attending their English classes. The results were amazing! The students raised their reading levels by a grade level in four months! I had to see this for myself, so I traveled to Naperville in the winter of 2007.

I saw firsthand how these students benefited from physical education class. The English teacher was also allowing students to move in the English classroom. There was coordinated and purposeful movement that incorporated learning concepts. The students were on step boxes and reciting vocabulary words; they were stationed on exercise bicycles while reading; every child was moving and learning. I knew I had to bring this to Charleston.

I had the perfect school and the perfect teacher to make this happen. Lindsey Beck was the physical education teacher at Mitchell Elementary School, a Title 1 school located in urban Charleston. Our plan was to build an exercise room that would have television screens throughout the room. All of these screens would be linked to a main computer. The teacher would develop lessons and put them on a flash drive that would then be displayed on the television screens. The students would rotate from one piece of equipment to the next while reading and reciting the televised lessons. We called this first room the AMX room—All Minds Exercising.

The only problem was that we had no money, no equipment, no televisions—not even a room. After the principal dedicated a room to these efforts, we spent the next six months raising $30,000. We received small grants from local medical associations; we canvassed local businesses and banks and had small fund-raisers. Purchasing the equipment was my biggest concern. The equipment had to be sized for elementary school children and fall within our budget. I priced equipment in all the major catalogs that would meet our needs. I priced televisions, computers, floor tiles, and paint.

After searching for one month, I came across a fitness equipment manufacturer located 10 miles outside Charleston. He built children's fitness equipment. I contacted Kidsfit and spoke directly with the owner, Ed Pinney. I asked if he would meet me at Mitchell and allow me to tell him my idea. We met in the room that we had been given. I laid out my vision of the brain room. He said that he would provide exactly what I wanted—a stair stepper placed here, a treadmill located there, a seated rowing machine in the corner, and a stationary bicycle. My mind was trying to tally the costs. I asked, "How much?" He said that it would cost us nothing. He felt the concept was unique, and he would furnish the equipment gratis as long as he could use the Mitchell room as a showcase. Thus was born the first Kidsfit kinesthetic classroom.

In the fall of 2009, Charleston County School District (CCSD) was awarded a Carol M. White Physical Education Grant (PEP Grant). The scope of the grant included building eight more brain rooms in CCSD schools that were designed much like the Mitchell Elementary room. This included building a brain room at Stall High School. The principal there was a huge advocate of movement in the classroom.

The idea for the brain room came from Jean Blades Moize, Dan Connor the principal, and myself. It would become the first NeuroNasium. This would be a resource room that was manned by a dedicated teacher. She would collaborate with the classroom teacher who wanted to use the brain room. They would develop a lesson plan that would incorporate their subject and the exercise equipment and movement stations: two teachers, two sets of eyes all intensely focused on learning and moving. The first kinesthetic desks were designed for this classroom.

Ed and I had always talked of how to build classrooms that had no stationary desks, so he designed and built elliptical machines, bicycles, and steppers that had desktops. The first prototypes were placed in the Stall High School brain room. Schools from other areas in the county began to hear about the brain room at Stall. Tours were provided, and soon other Charleston schools were asking for kinesthetic desks. Primarily schools would place one or two in a classroom, and they would be used for "problem" kids, until Stacey Schoecraft, a fifth-grade teacher at Pinckney Elementary (and author of Teaching Through Movement: Setting Up Your Kinesthetic Classroom*), decided to furnish her entire classroom with kinesthetic desks. She saw the value in having every student in a desk that provided a movement option. Stacey's classroom was hailed as the first fully Kidsfit kinesthetic classroom in the United States.*

Neuroscience over the past decade has provided the evidence that movement changes the brain, body, behaviors, and the ability to learn. Is there another educational strategy that can make the same claim? Let's free our students from "educational incarceration." The kinesthetic classroom is being heralded as that new strategy in education.

Today, Kidsfit has developed more than 200 different types of fitness products for children, selling direct nationwide and providing distributers in five continents. By sticking close to their mission, "Changing the future for all children, by increasing their health, wellness and education through movement," Kidsfit has become the leading developer and manufacturer of youth fitness equipment in the United States, including cardio fitness equipment, climbing walls, and obstacle courses.

In 2012 Kidsfit began working with a team of brain research experts, educational consultants, and classroom teachers to develop a new way for children to learn and interact in their classrooms. What came out of the research and classroom testing was a line of kinesthetic, motion desks and tables that allow children to be in motion while they learn! This is not exercise equipment—this is an entire teaching methodology that utilizes standing tables, motion chairs, and numerous simple movements that allow teachers to actually have more control in their classrooms while providing a classroom experience that is far more conducive to learning than traditional methods. This equipment comes with formal training and classroom certifications for schools and after-school learning centers, kinesthetic classroom furniture, action-based learning labs, and home and active play custom products. Kidsfit kinesthetic classroom products have reached 47 states since 2014.

Source: Photo courtesy of Kidsfit.

Source: Photo courtesy of Kidsfit.

Source: Photo courtesy of Kidsfit.

Source: Photo courtesy of Kidsfit.

CHAPTER SUMMARY

- The idea of using movement and physical activity in the classroom has evolved, and the very best results can be seen in a three-pronged approach: (1) using movement in the classroom according to the framework that is provided herein that becomes a natural part of the school culture, (2) making aerobic activity, physical education, and physical fitness a district-wide priority, and (3) creating the modern classroom through the use of specialized furniture that allows students to be physically engaged throughout their schooling experience.
- In 2010 the CDC produced a report that solidified physical activity's place in America's schools and classrooms.
- Research continues to support the use of movement and physical activity during the school day, recess, and physical education.
- It is important that teachers stay abreast of at least a broad overview of research that connects various forms of movement and aerobic activity and learning.
- More and more colleges and universities are offering courses and programs based in movement and physical activity.
- The Alief Independent School District in Houston, Texas, and PSD in Pottstown, Pennsylvania, are two examples of the many school

districts that have successfully implemented movement and wellness programs and created a culture of movement within their districts.

- Action-based learning labs—physically active rooms in combination with academic content—are quickly becoming part of the educational landscape.
- The modern classroom is changing after a long period of stagnation from the standpoint of furniture. Kinesthetic furniture can now be found in 47 states and on five continents and is a growing trend in how students experience school and learning.
- Classrooms, schools, and school districts are creating a multipronged approach to movement and physical activity. By using physical activity in the classroom during the school day, before- and after-school movement and wellness programs, fitness-oriented physical education classes (that are at times positioned in the schedule to support subject areas), action-based learning labs, and kinesthetic classroom furniture are improving the learning experience for students by leaps and bounds.

TIPS FOR THE STAFF DEVELOPER

Always have several pieces of research that help support your presentation by connecting it to practical application. It is also important to understand the broad approach and culture that can be created through different types of movement, physical activity, and physical fitness available to a school district.

3

The Brain/Body
Connection

Nine Thoughts to Move By

⇨ What are nine thoughts or phrases that are important for teachers to understand and that make information about how the brain prefers to learn accessible and applicable?

In *The Kinesthetic Classroom: Teaching and Learning Through Movement,* we began Chapter 2 with the following:

> One hundred years from now, historians may look on current life as an age where the exciting possibilities of the brain-body relationship were finally realized. Each year brings new evidence supporting the notion that the two have been mistakenly assumed as separate entities. The fact is that they flow to and through each other, as an extension and a reflection of the other's will. Time will tell how this understanding might affect medicine and education: how doctors diagnose and how teachers design learning. . . . Our understanding of the brain-body relationship may indeed be the

most exciting scientific advance of the 21st century. It is basic to the human experience and has largely been left on the shelf as a viable educational tool that enhances both teaching and learning. (Lengel & Kuczala, 2010, pp. 16–17)

Almost a decade later, we feel no differently. Medicine has become more accepting of stress reduction and management activities—in particular meditation. Its benefits long known and now thoroughly studied, meditation calms both the brain and body and allows for a different perspective on everyday living. It's even being used in schools as a way to reduce stress and improve classroom management. Closely related, the term "mindfulness" has become quite a buzz word in education and rightfully so. It brings together the brain and body to be able to experience the moment without distraction. Mindfulness, a brain/body art, has the ability to increase attention, executive function, and emotional regulation and to decrease stress and anxiety—all things that add to a quality emotional environment that produces more quality learning. Movement itself often engages mindfulness. When students are involved in thoughtful, purposeful, and engaging physical activity where direction is given and attention needed, focus on the moment happens naturally, reducing stress and raising engagement and motivational levels. Students experience what we refer to as "mindful movement."

As you ready yourself for becoming a Kinesthetic Educator, understanding how the brain prefers to learn becomes paramount. The brain/body connection is alive and well in classrooms. It always has been and always will be. The more teachers understand and recognize its presence, the more they can influence it to everyone's cognitive advantage. In our reflection in preparing this chapter, we made a decision to make it as practical as possible for the classroom teacher. Instead of presenting a more standard chapter on the brain and how it is reflected in movement (e.g., brain parts, memory systems, and neural networks), we decided to offer nine phrases that we think are brief, practical, memorable, and more likely to engage educators in their understanding of the relationship between important cognitive principles and using movement and physical activity as a matter of regular classroom practice. We think that all educators should have a thorough understanding of how the brain learns to create a classroom that offers the most opportunity for a child to learn and grow but that is a much larger conversation than just movement, physical activity, and physical fitness. If you are interested in such a resource, David Sousa's *How the Brain Learns* (2017) is essential for your library. During the writing of this book, his fifth edition of *How the Brain Learns* was released. It is at the top of our reading list.

For now, we've trimmed the information to what we feel is manageable for you to take on while creating a kinesthetic classroom. These thoughts, or statements, are what have stood out to us over the past 10 years as important for teachers to understand the whys of making movement and physical activity integral to the classroom experience. It also makes a small portion of cognitive research palatable for everyday use. They have also been very important to our graduate courses, keynotes, and professional development—as educators have been able to easily translate their meaning to their own practice.

1. LEARNING DOESN'T HAPPEN FROM THE NECK UP: IT HAPPENS FROM THE FEET UP

A local high school recently asked Mike to speak to students at its annual career day. The invitation was a return engagement that came after the publication of *The Kinesthetic Classroom: Teaching and Learning Through Movement.*

As the first to speak that day, I was positioned onstage waiting for the students to file in and didn't initially notice the young woman standing on the floor motioning me over at stage left. But when she did catch my eye, I walked over, and the young woman immediately stated her purpose.

"Weren't you here last year?" she said.

"Yes, I gave the keynote," I replied, a little flattered that she remembered.

"I thought so," she told me with some excitement. "I remember because you taught us how to learn SAT vocabulary words using our bodies, and you taught us how to remember the meaning of words like obstinate."

"And why did you remember that word?" I asked.

She smiled, made a fist with her right hand, and began tapping it against her head. Then she said, "Hard-headed." Next, she used her hands to push away from her body and said, "Unyielding."

She laughed, told me she was looking forward to my talk, and then turned on her heels to scurry back to her waiting friends.

I recount this story because it provides a clear example of the most important underlying principle of this book—that movement enhances our brain's ability to learn and, more specifically as this story demonstrates, moves what we learn from temporary memory to permanent storage for later recall. More than a year had passed between the day my curious student had participated in the short demonstration activity I gave at my talk, yet she recalled exactly what she learned. For me, this is the perfect illustration of how the brain/body connection enhances the learning process.

It is common that participants in one of our professional development sessions learn about the parts of a neuron for several different purposes. The dendrite, nucleus, axon, myelin sheath, and neurotransmitters all become very familiar to them after about a five-minute lesson. We also discuss the hippocampus at different junctures throughout the training but really don't learn about it using physical means. Eventually, I'll raise my right arm and wiggle my fingers, and participants respond with "dendrites!" I'll point to my palm—"Nucleus!" After going through all the parts using my hand and brief definitions, I shock them with a question—"Who in here can tell me even one function of the hippocampus?" I get blank looks. Kiddingly I say, "But I've discussed it, I went over it, and it'll be on the test on Friday!" They chuckle and quickly realize my point. Because we've used our bodies to learn a concept, it becomes that much more memorable and retrievable.

Also consider learning when students are sitting. How they feel and how comfortable they are make a difference in learning. The body always impacts learning because of the brain/body connection. Recognizing this fact will produce better results on many levels.

2. EMOTIONAL ENVIRONMENT SETS THE STAGE FOR INTELLECTUAL ACHIEVEMENT

Sylwester (1995) says that emotion is important in education—it drives attention, which in turn drives learning and memory. Learning occurs more easily in environments free from threat or intimidation (Sousa, 2017). Learning is easier to store, remember, and retrieve if it has an emotional base. Research on positive teacher-student relationships shows an increase in academic achievement. Conversely, when the relationship is negative, academic achievement declines. Research shows the same findings when it comes to supportive, positive school environments.

The bottom line is that when a student feels safe, cared for, and supported, he or she is more likely to have an outlook that produces motivation and academic achievement. In creating a safe home for the brain, we are also setting the stage for school-related, responsible, intellectual risk-taking. Students need to know that it is OK, in fact sometimes desired, to be wrong. Being incorrect provides free information about what not to do next time! Different students experience different levels of risk in school all day long. Different people are more comfortable in different settings and classes. The more safe and respectful the environment, the greater childrens' willingness to take a risk, in the knowledge that it's OK to be incorrect and grow and learn from the experience.

Movement, especially during cohesion activities, can help provide the desired environment to take risk and achieve. Movement activities are often done in pairs or groups—and naturally produce laughter and build community and teamwork.

3. AS FAR AS LEARNING AND THE BRAIN IS CONCERNED, SHORTER IS USUALLY BETTER

Working memory, whose activity mostly happens in the frontal lobe, has capacity limits, especially when dealing with new information that has little or no relevance to the learner. The hippocampus, crucial to the conversion of working memory to long-term memory, has a limited capacity and can be easily overwhelmed. Imagine this part of the brain being the size of a paper cup. Teachers often try to fill this paper cup with information that would fit into a large pitcher!

Built-in brain breaks and time for processing academic content are essential to the learning process. Movement can provide a necessary break from learning and actually make the entire process more efficient.

Refocusing attention may just be the most useful benefit of movement. Some have referred to it as "magical." Upon finishing movement activities with students and/or teachers, it is normal for them to feel more focused and attentive. It's simply working with the brain instead of against it. When implementing exercise and fitness challenges, an educator can refocus his or her students' attention in seconds. For example, asking students to stand and perform 10 jumping jacks is a quick way to give the brain a burst of fresh oxygen while refocusing it for further learning.

4. FOR INFORMATION TO MOVE FROM WORKING MEMORY TO LONG-TERM MEMORY, SOMETHING HAS TO HAPPEN TO THE INFORMATION OR TO THE EXPERIENCE

Long-term memory is the essential goal of all teaching. With some reflection you'll realize the truth in this statement! We want students to be able to retain information they learn in school to recall it for assessment purposes, to use next month or next year in school, or to use throughout life. Long-term memory is the reason schools exist, yet so often we teach students what they need to know but not how to remember it, which is critical to long-term memory formation. According to Lee Oberparleiter (2004), unless you, as a teacher, teach students *how* to remember what you want them to remember, they will continue to flounder.

The problem with this scenario is that the brain is not set up to remember everything it engages. That would be information overload, and the brain is purposefully set up to lose most information before it reaches long-term memory. Short-term memory is divided into immediate memory and working memory, both of which have very restrictive time and capacity limits (Sousa, 2017). The objective is for information to pass through both short-term memory components and move into long-term memory storage. This is easier said than done. Without a profound sense of interest or emotional connection, information can easily be forgotten. Here are some suggestions for something to happen to the information or experience (Oberparleiter, 2004):

- Find a pattern.
- Make connections.
- Develop personal interest.

- Associate it with prior experience.
- Engage emotionally.
- Practice it.

Making learning physical also qualifies for the list. Learning content through movement or kinesthetic activity is something happening to the information in a powerful way that the brain prefers. The brain operates from concrete experience. Nothing is more concrete than using movement to learn or review a concept.

5. MEANING MAKING IS STATE DEPENDENT

State management is the management of the brain/body emotional state of your students. It is a concept that is often unfamiliar to teachers yet may be the most critical factor in the teaching and learning process. In a traditional classroom students are seated, quiet, and orderly (we hope). The teacher goes about his or her lesson that often involves lecture, listening, reading, writing, reviewing, and possibly some discussion. Teaching is a very involved profession that takes years to master and requires many skills that are often learned along the way. On top of everything a teacher must know and do, we are also asking that you add the state management of your students to the list.

Why is this so important? Eric Jensen (2000) tells us that a student's learning state has a great influence on the meaning that is created during the learning process. He says that meaning making is state dependent (see Figure 3.1). Therefore, if a student has a positive learning state when material is being taught, the student has a better opportunity to make connections and understand the concepts and the information he or she is learning. Sousa (2017) indicates that meaning and sense are two nonnegotiable criteria for content retention. We stated earlier that a teacher's practice is all about long-term memory. Interestingly, of the two criteria, meaning is more significant. One of the best tools you have at your disposal to manage state is movement. The next time you see attention waning, yawns prevailing, body language that says "I am bored, uninterested, or tired because I've been sitting all period," stop what you are doing and, at the very least, have your students stand. Preferably, you'll take a moment to increase blood and oxygen flow to your student's brains by providing a quick brain break or boost. This will quickly manage the state in the room and give students a much better chance of finding meaning in the content in which they are about to engage. Music is also an effective state manager, especially when combined with movement. Imagine sitting bored and tired, and all of a sudden you hear the theme from *Rocky* played through blaring speakers. Would your state change? Absolutely! I'll bet your state just now changed simply by reading about it and having the song in your head.

Figure 3.1   Movement, State Management, and Meaning

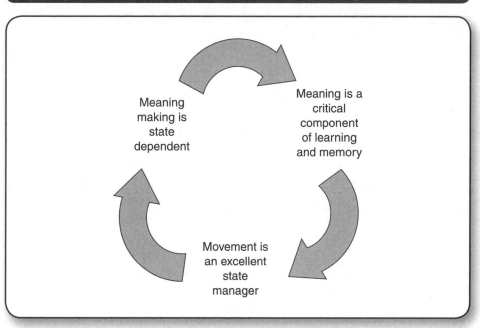

Meaning making is state dependent

Meaning is a critical component of learning and memory

Movement is an excellent state manager

Tony Robbins, a motivational inspiration to the masses, is a king state manager because he understands the science behind it and knows the advantage it provides him. Attending one of his seminars is a giant lesson in state management. At his core, Tony is a teacher. While in his classroom you stand on chairs, scream, dance, sing, discuss, work in teams, set goals, and learn incredibly well! In a typical day at a Business Mastery seminar, an attendee begins standing in line for the best seat possible at 7:00 a.m. The day begins at 8:00 a.m. and does not finish until around 10:00 p.m. with a one hour-long break during the middle. It's incredible to experience. Many who attend say they could keep going for hours. Why? It all boils down to Tony's, and Tony's team's, ability to manage state. There would be no other way to do it.

Tony also talks about "physiology changing your psychology," meaning that the way you hold yourself physically (stand tall, head up, shoulders back, smile on your face, etc.) can instantly change your state and influence your psychology for the better. In one of the most viewed TED Talks ever—"Your Body Language Shapes Who You Are" (see https://www.ted.com/talks/amy_cuddy_your_body_language_shapes_who_you_are)—social psychologist Amy Cuddy shows how "power posing," standing in a posture of confidence, even when we don't feel confident—can affect testosterone and cortisol levels in the brain. This information offers students the ability to self-manage state and change their psychology through physiology.

Making meaning that is intimately connected to long-term memory formation is affected by the state of the learner, a daily consideration in your professional practice.

6. THE STUDENTS WHO DO THE DOING AND WHO DO THE TALKING DO THE LEARNING

This statement is self-explanatory. By now you understand how valuable a learning tool your body is and how effective movement can be in the teaching and learning process. On some level, much of what we learn happens by doing. Although it is not always possible to have students learn by doing, when it is information it can become instantly permanent. Think about your own profession or any other for that matter. When did you really get better at your trade—during your undergraduate classes or when you student taught? When did you feel competent and effective at teaching—during your first year of teaching? Third? Tenth? The answer varies dramatically, but every teacher gets better through practice, with experience, and by doing. At some point, you have to take it out of the book, off the PowerPoint, and away from lecturing and listening and make it three-dimensional, practical, and real. The same can be said of your students. The more they get to experience and do, the more they will learn. It's simply what the brain prefers.

Of course, it is critical for the brain (and student) to talk about learning. As just noted, meaning and sense are two nonnegotiable criteria for content retention. Sense and meaning can be very personal items. What is meaningful to one individual may not be meaningful to another; what makes no sense to one person makes perfect sense to the next. When students stand, partner with another student, and discuss their learning, they now have the opportunity to assign sense and/or meaning to the content, providing yet another opportunity for long-term storage.

7. THE BRAIN IS ALWAYS CREATING A LEARNING ADDRESS FOR WHERE IT LEARNS SOMETHING

Can you recall a memory that will be etched in your brain forever? We all have them. It most likely has a strong emotional tag. The fact that it even is in your memory bank is due to the emotional impression of the memory and the importance given to it by the amygdala, which encodes emotional messages. Within that same memory, can you recall where you were and actually pull out details of the environment? If so, this is due to episodic or environmental memory controlled by the hippocampus.

During a learning episode, an environmental address is created in connection with the data. In other words, the brain makes note of where it is when it learns something. When movement is used to learn a concept, a unique environmental note is made by the brain, making the information easier to recall. Through movement and physical activity, it is possible for the brain to create unique environmental pictures of learning, which can enhance students' abilities to recall information later.

8. MOVEMENT MEETS NEEDS AND CREATES MOTIVATION

From our perspective a teacher's biggest hurdle on a daily basis is not curriculum, not assessment, and not planning; it is student motivation. It is a dilemma that will never cease to exist, but there are ways to increase your chances of creating a motivated environment and student through the use of movement and physical activity. We often ask participants in our professional development sessions, "Have you been more motivated today when you've been moving or when we've been talking?" The answer is always a resounding "moving!" Of course, we are built to move. It is natural to our existence and is often how we learn and relate to the world around us. Motivation is a natural by-product of an engaging, active, movement-oriented classroom.

William Glasser's (1998) *Choice Theory* and internal control psychology offers us some insight into how this might play out in the classroom. He identifies the following as basic human needs:

- Survival
- Belonging
- Power
- Freedom
- Fun

These needs are often not addressed in a school setting, causing behavior and academic problems as well as frustration for teachers and students. In *Activating the Desire to Learn*, author Bob Sullo (2007) writes:

The good news is that we can create learning environments that foster the motivation that makes education a joyful enterprise. Internal control psychology teaches us that that we are driven to connect, to be competent, to make choices, to have fun, and to be safe. Structure a classroom and school where those five needs are regularly met, and you will inspire motivation that fuels academic excellence and exemplary behavior. (p. 156)

Upon closer examination, movement can help meet all these needs in schools and classrooms. Is it the only way to achieve this end? Of course not, but our framework can be implemented, with some effort, immediately at almost no cost. When students are allowed to engage in the learning process through movement, it is possible to meet survival needs, especially for those kinesthetically preferred students who sit nearly all day long or for students with a learning difference such as ADHD, where movement becomes crucial. Schools are restrictive places by nature, so allowing movement in the classroom provides a newfound sense of freedom as students are allowed to move about the room in a purposeful manner. The need for power is met through enhanced competence because of matched learning style and more accessibility to content. Implicit learning, which represents differentiation by learning profile, is utilized, thus reaching far more learners than a traditional model. Movement-oriented classroom cohesion activities build trust, which is essential to creating a sustainable home for the brain. Many brain breaks, boosts, and energizers, and review and teaching content activities, also engage more than one student at a time, helping to build trust and community. Finally, when the decision is made to use more movement in the classroom, the learning and environment become fun. In turn, students want to take part in learning instead of feeling disengaged.

9. REMEMBER, STUDENTS ARE ALWAYS PAYING ATTENTION, PROBABLY JUST NOT TO YOU

Don't be offended; it's just a survival mechanism of the brain. Every teacher in a classroom and every administrator in a meeting has witnessed yawning, glazed-over eyes, and staring out the window. As previously described, using movement can be a quick and easy way to bring someone's focus and attention back where it belongs. This is especially important for students dealing with attention deficit disorder (ADD) and ADHD. Research suggests that a lack of movement can cause or contribute to the symptoms of hyperactivity. Children with hyperactivity disorders who run before class have shown significant behavior improvement to the point of having their medication reduced if running occurred on a daily basis (Putnam, 2003).

CHAPTER SUMMARY

- As you ready yourself for becoming a Kinesthetic Educator, understanding how the brain prefers to learn becomes paramount.
- There are nine thoughts or phrases that are important for teachers to understand about how the brain prefers to learn.
- Learning doesn't happen from the neck up: it happens from the feet up.

- Emotional environment sets the stage for intellectual achievement.
- As far as learning and the brain is concerned, shorter is usually better.
- For information to move from working memory to long-term memory, something has to happen to the information or the experience.
- Meaning making is state dependent.
- The students who do the doing and who do the talking do the learning.
- The brain is always creating a learning address for where it learns something.
- Movement meets needs and creates motivation.
- Remember, students are always paying attention, probably just not to you.

TIPS FOR THE STAFF DEVELOPER

Although these nine thoughts seem like intellectual pursuits as they are, there is always a way to make them experiential for your audience. For example, you could take audience members through state management activities or use the block partnering activity from Chapter 9 to emphasize Phrase 5.

PART 2

READY

Structuring the Environment

4

Building and Managing a Kinesthetic Environment

> ⇨ Building: How can controlled movement with purpose affect behaviors in my classroom?
>
> ⇨ Building: What steps should I take to build my kinesthetic environment?
>
> ⇨ Managing: What are effective classroom management strategies I can use in a kinesthetic environment?
>
> ⇨ Building and Managing: How can I take it to the next level?

BUILDING: HOW CAN CONTROLLED MOVEMENT WITH PURPOSE AFFECT BEHAVIORS IN MY CLASSROOM?

The idea of managing classroom behavior while students are moving to learn may be intimidating for some teachers and administrators. Educators' personalities and past experiences will greatly affect their comfort levels regarding movement. If you were active throughout your life, perhaps participated in or coached sports, you may be more accepting of the concept that a kinesthetic environment is ideal for learning and enhancing cognition. In opposition, if you had limited experiences with movement, or even negative incidents, then movement in the classroom may not make sense to you. It is imperative to keep in mind that using kinesthetic teaching methodologies in your classroom is about both you and your students exploring and experiencing positive feelings about movement—where academic achievements are increased, social connections are made, and all feel good about themselves.

By nature, countless teachers love structure, organization, and control. The concept of movement in an academic environment can make these educators feel a loss of power. This is a myth. A teacher who uses movement activities effectively to enhance academic achievement will exercise what is referred to as "controlled movement with purpose." This means that the educator has a well-organized environment that maintains structure and discipline where optimal learning is the result. The first step to building a kinesthetic environment is to realize you will have control while students are learning and using movement to master the content. Yes, students may be laughing and having fun, noise level may be slightly increased (not necessarily), and energy levels will be lifted, but doesn't this sound like a perfect recipe for learning? Somewhere along the way, we have linked the idea that a learning environment does not include laughter and enjoyment. This philosophy is in opposition to meeting our basic human needs. A key aspect of learning is having the motivation to do so. Motivation sustains behavior, gets students moving, points them in the right direction, and keeps them on this path (Ormrod, 2014). Building a kinesthetic environment provides this motivation. Students will not only enjoy the activities; they will also crave and request them. Once they experience that fun and learning go hand in hand, why wouldn't this become their learning preference? In conjunction, it will also become educators' and administrators' preference as well, as the love of learning spreads and grows. Ultimately this can improve attendance in a school district and build a cohesive environment that everyone will enjoy.

If experience is limited, it is understandable that teachers and administrators might feel that movement in a classroom might increase discipline problems. Although this is a possibility, it is no more likely than problems occurring with any other instructional methodology. In fact, when used purposefully and carefully, movement can lead to a more focused, productive, and disciplined classrooms. When Braniff (2011) explored movement activities with fourth-grade students, she found evidence that students were eager to move, and the activities impacted classroom management, alertness, and attention.

Once you take the position of becoming a Kinesthetic Educator and you realize you will have controlled movement with purpose, you must prepare yourself for the various personalities of your students and their current mentalities of a traditional learning environment. Many students have connected learning to sitting in a seat while listening to lectures and completing worksheets, all while complying with a teacher-directed environment. Although these methodologies still play their role, they may stifle creativity, advanced problem solving, and critical thinking. Initially, be prepared that some students will not choose kinesthetic activities as their preference for learning in an academic setting. They have already built a comfort level with a methodology that is very different from moving to learn. However, research and common sense tell us that students, like adults, don't like to sit and listen all day either. We need to create a balance; kinesthetic teaching combined with other teaching methodologies is an irrefutable solution.

Kinesthetic activities are not only a fun means of learning, but they are in line with the physical nature of the body. All bodies are designed to move, and unfortunately, both societal changes and education are moving in the opposite direction of our bodily needs and requirements. The body has obvious, positive responses to movement. When engaged in physical activity, people of all ages typically experience pleasure. As a result of movement, the body releases neurotransmitters (such as serotonin and dopamine) and hormones (such as endorphins and adrenalin), all of which promote pleasure and excitement. Therefore, if not initially, students will ultimately be motivated to move in a classroom setting.

BUILDING: WHAT STEPS SHOULD I TAKE TO BUILD MY KINESTHETIC ENVIRONMENT?

Safety and Ease of Movement

Once you have taken the position to become a Kinesthetic Educator and accepted that you will have controlled movement with an academic purpose, it is now time to consider your next essential steps and their delivery. Initially you must acknowledge that you will need to have some patience through this process. The chance of perfecting your kinesthetic environment techniques and strategies without some failure is unrealistic. There will be a trial-and-error phase that you will need to constantly develop and grow. Quite honestly, this will continue throughout your entire career as you master your skill and refine your techniques. Embrace this as a positive aspect of movement as it is ever-changing and dynamic, which is exactly what your students crave.

Your primary responsibility as a Kinesthetic Educator is to consider the safety of your students prior to moving them in a classroom environment. Safety is unquestionably the most important aspect of classroom management for the Kinesthetic Educator. Scan your classroom for areas of concern. Consider the following:

- Are there pointy objects or jagged corners?
- What is breakable?
- Are there uneven floors or objects that can be hazardous?
- Is the ceiling height a concern?
- What about technology? Are there safe places in the room to store expensive items?

- How will I adjust my activities based on what my students are wearing?
- What rules and expectations will I set?
- How will I transition my students from movement to seat?
- How can I set up my classroom that will allow for optimal movement in a safe environment?

The safety of your classroom needs your serious consideration. Educators and administrators alike may not believe they have enough space in their classrooms to promote movement activities. This is simply not true. Although a smaller space may present challenges, many movement activities require very little space. Additionally, activities that appear to require a larger area can be modified to fit any given environment. This often requires creative thinking on the educators' part, but it is both feasible and safe with a controlled-movement-with-purpose mentality. Furthermore, educators may be concerned with injuries that may occur during movement activities. It is undeniable that accidents may occur whenever we move our bodies in a classroom or anywhere else for that matter. However, we cannot spend our lives sitting in a chair afraid to move because we might get hurt. That is not a realistic way to live, nor is it a fair way to teach. If our goal is optimal learning, we must use superior teaching methodologies to achieve this. Safety is and will always be the top priority with a Kinesthetic Educator; therefore, you must continually maintain a secure environment. Although some may believe injuries can increase with movement in smaller spaces, this is not accurate in a controlled environment. The smaller the space, the slower the speeds of movement; hence, injuries should be both minimal and minor. These are two crucial points in regard to safety in a kinesthetic environment.

Whenever possible, a Kinesthetic Educator should consider the setup of his or her classroom to allow for efficiency and ease of movement. If you travel from room to room, you are limited with options. However, if you have one space with the ability to move tables, chairs, desks, and technology equipment, you are fortunate to have the opportunity to make the space fit your needs. A horseshoe or U-shaped variation may be the most effective classroom arrangement for teaching and learning through movement. Another consideration that may be useful is desks grouped in pods; this will also lend itself effectively to class cooperation activities and discussion groups. Classrooms that have traditional rows are not optimal for movement; however, movement activities can be modified to accommodate this arrangement as well.

Introducing Movement

Your delivery to your students about becoming a Kinesthetic Educator is immense. Not only will you be teaching through movement, but your students will be learning through movement as they become a kinesthetic class. Both you and your students will work together to build this environment and elevate success. Therefore, it becomes the educator's initial responsibility to convince students that movement not only belongs in a classroom setting but is ideal. Express to your students what factors convinced you take this position. Share with them the whys before they even have the opportunity to ask. The research is not only profound but includes common sense. Many students love to challenge you and question your requests, techniques, and strategies. Adopt a preventive approach to this by sharing your knowledge and excitement about movement right from the start. A Kinesthetic Educator develops a passion for movement that trickles down to the students. Show your enthusiasm and share your energy for this profound teaching methodology. Positivity is contagious; allow your students to develop their love for kinesthetic learning as you grow together through this process.

After building eagerness and anticipation of becoming a kinesthetic classroom, the teacher's second responsibility is to discuss the seriousness of safety with the students and how movement in a classroom environment may differ from the gymnasium or a larger space. Mention the idea of both bodies and objects and moving around their given space with desks, tables, and technology as potential obstacles. One suggestion is to have students take the following two tests.

1. "The Driver's Test"

- Students imagine their bodies as cars.
- In a given space, they choose their speed and direction for one minute as they move around the room.
- Observe how students choose various speeds while analyzing their space and surroundings.
- If a car (body) gets into an accident with another car or object, the car must be parked for driving out of control.
- Give directions appropriate for your age level, and discuss that accidents can happen even when cars are under control. Discuss that safe speeds (never faster than a walk) will result in minimal, minor accidents only.
- This is also a good time to mention noise levels during movement activities as students need to keep their horns (mouths) quiet.

2. "The Ball Pass Test"

- Have students get a partner and a ball (or safe object).
- In a given space, they will throw their ball/object back and forth with their partners for one minute.
- Observe throwing and catching skills and control.
- If a ball/object is flying across the room, the student who threw it does not pass the test and must take a seat to consider his or her actions. The test must be retaken at a different time.

- Give directions appropriate for your age level, and discuss that balls/object must always be thrown gently with care. Hard, aggressive passes will never be tolerated.
- Discuss that skill levels vary, and inaccurate throws and drops may occur; however, control must always be present.

These two tests will prove to you and your students that both body and ball movement can be very safe in your classroom environment. You also now have set clear expectations to the speed at which students should move and the minimal force that should be applied while throwing objects in a smaller space. These tests provide a basis for upcoming movement activities that you should refer back to on a regular basis. Furthermore, you have now created an opportunity to discuss the consequences that will be given when students are not moving their bodies safely or throwing objects cautiously. The standards you set here and your ability to enforce them are arguably the most important aspect of safety in respect to classroom management.

The next step is to teach and master your classroom routines linked to movement. This includes, but may not be limited to, transitioning from movement to seat, moving desks, and getting into partners or groups. Some of these routines may vary from activity to activity; however, the more consistent you can be, the better opportunity for efficiency when prepping for and using movement in the classroom. Transitioning from movement to seat and moving desks when necessary may be two techniques that you may want to keep constant throughout the year. Let's face it; if precious time is lost when preparing for movement or concluding movement activities, it can make the activity feel like a burden. Hence, movement is connected to lost time in situations where every second counts. Make all routines clear, simple, and quick. Literally, use a stopwatch to time students to see how efficient they can be. Set goals and expectations that must be met before proceeding forward with movement activities in your classroom. Students will respond to these challenges and take ownership of using movement for teaching and learning.

Set guidelines for proper attire for movement activities in your classroom. It is difficult to be consistent here because all movement activities are different. For example, sneakers are not a requirement for many movements you will use in your classroom. However, for some activities, sneakers are a must. You will have to address each lesson individually while having a backup plan if students are not prepared for kinesthetic learning in the classroom. You may assign students a different role in the activity or have an alternative lesson or activity plan. If this becomes too difficult a challenge in your given circumstance, focus on movement activities that will work as long as students are following the school dress code and guidelines.

Finally, once safety factors and consequences are understood and routines are mastered, you are ready to move forward as a Kinesthetic

Educator. You are now in a situation where you can focus on how you will use movement on a day-to-day basis. One vital consideration is to start slow and simple. We will address how to do this as we move forward in the book. However, even as you begin your quest with movements that have a high probability for success, you still must consider your preventive strategies for potential classroom management challenges. These proactive techniques may play a strategic role in building your kinesthetic environment.

MANAGING: WHAT ARE EFFECTIVE CLASSROOM MANAGEMENT STRATEGIES I CAN USE IN A KINESTHETIC ENVIRONMENT?

 Preventative

To have successful classroom management in a kinesthetic environment, it is critical to include proactive strategies that may prevent challenges from occurring. Having effective classroom management strategies and techniques is a continual challenge that teachers face despite the teaching methodology that they use. What works with one student may not work with another. A technique used successfully one day may be ineffective with that same student the next. In many incidences there is no rhyme or reason of how to manage classroom behavior without fail. Diverse viewpoints exist about what strategies yield the most success when it comes to classroom management. However, the key is to have as many strategies as possible and to try to figure out which works best in a given situation with each student. This period of trial and error is never-ending as students personalities are changing as they grow and develop. Additionally, educators also need to consider their own character and beliefs regarding management. Patience is required as you find your own comfort level and develop your strategies and techniques.

To recognize preventive classroom management strategies, visualize your students participating in movement activities, and ask, "What potential problems could arise?" Consider students who will challenge you or the activity you have asked them to engage in. Ask yourself what preventive strategies or techniques could be used to prevent problems before they begin. Mentally, go through the steps of each activity a few times while trying to predict the challenges that may arise. Also, prepare yourself for situations that will have less-than-desirable outcomes and possibly fail to succeed. It is impossible to get everything right every time. Effective management of student behaviors during movement activities is a skill that develops as you continue to experiment with various methods. Here are 10 classroom management strategies to consider prior to getting started.

1. Define expectations.
   - Set your standards.
   - Keep them clear and simple.
   - Discuss consequences for off-task or inappropriate behavior.

2. Use proximity.
   - Stand closer to students you are concerned about.
   - Make sure they are paying attention when directions are given.

3. Have students repeat directions.
   - Prior to starting have students repeat the directions of the activity to you or a friend.
   - Ask students to repeat examples of off-task behavior and consequences to follow.

4. Use cues.
   - Keep them short and succinct.
   - Use a step-by-step approach such as 1, 2, and 3 to order the events or procedures.

5. Choose certain students to model the activity.
   - Ask students who display off-task behavior to demonstrate the activity.
   - Consider making them captions or give them a leadership role.

6. Use partners effectively when necessary.
   - Assign partners who will balance each other with difficult classes.
   - Use "Choose your own partner" as a reward.

7. Provide time limits.
   - Set limits with expectations and consequences.
   - Keep time limits short.

8. Start small.
   - Use activities from "Set" to build comfort and efficiency.
   - Choose activities that are performed alone before involving a partner.

9. Use controlled, directed movements first.
   - Stay clear of creative movements until comfort is built.
   - Use movements with few directions that will have a high success rate.

10. Move continuously.
    - Move around the outside of the room whenever possible.
    - Give continual feedback, and let students know you are watching.

Trying to predict potential problems with movement activities is an important step for the Kinesthetic Educator to take. This practice will help you improve the delivery of the directions for each activity while minimizing discipline problems. Teachers who are superior in utilizing preventative classroom management strategies typically have fewer behavioral challenges. Students know what the expectations are, and they rise to meet them. An educator who promotes structure, organization, and consistency will excel while managing a kinesthetic environment. Although preventive strategies are of the upmost importance, being able to react quickly and efficiently to challenging situations is equally as important.

Reactive

Behavioral challenges will and do occur in all classroom settings. Even the most skilled teachers find students who test them along with class rules and procedures. It is inevitable; students like to see what they are capable of getting away with. When students act out or misbehave, there is typically a reason for this behavior. Having the ability to react quickly and efficiently, without escalating a situation, is a critical skill for all teachers to develop, including the Kinesthetic Educator. The two main concerns regarding classroom management with the kinesthetic classroom are the unmotivated and the hypermotivated student. Preventive strategies must also be considered and executed with these students. However, reacting appropriately to a student who refuses to follow your directions will build or hinder the kinesthetic environment.

Understanding the Unmotivated Student

Students who are unmotivated in a kinesthetic environment are very difficult to manage. It is beneficial to establish a basis or reason for this lack of motivation. There are five potential explanations why students may show resistance toward movement. Making a personal connection with a student will give you some background knowledge and perhaps an understanding of his or her resistance toward movement. This will help when developing both preventive and reactive techniques for classroom management.

1. Poor self-perception
    o Fear of being unsuccessful
    o Afraid of looking foolish in front of peers
    o Concerned about their skill level
    o Teacher tip: Creating a positive environment with movement will be essential to build this particular student's motivation

2. Negative or limited past experiences
    o Unfamiliar with the joy that movement can bring
    o Haunting memories of the past

- ○ Feelings of inferiority
- ○ Teacher tip: Starting with simple activities that lead to immediate success will be very important to these students—positive feedback is also a key factor

3. Low or unclear expectations in the classroom
   - ○ Students rising to challenges set
   - ○ Students gaining trust in a teacher who believes in movement
   - ○ Keeping goals and standards high while asking for the students' best
   - ○ Teacher tip: Make a connection between movement and effort—believe in movement and your students while setting the bar high

4. Feeling pressure
   - ○ Negative feelings toward pressure
   - ○ Worried about how they will be viewed by peers
   - ○ Movement and stress linked together
   - ○ Teacher tip: Provide a positive, stress-free experience with movement so students feel accepted

5. Limited support in home or family environment
   - ○ Attitudes about movement from family members
   - ○ Unmotivated children from inactive families
   - ○ Families not believing in movement in the classroom
   - ○ Teacher tip: Be patient as you expose students to a new way of looking at movement

Preparing and Reacting to the Unmotivated Student

The elementary teacher will be presented with different challenges regarding the unmotivated student in movement activities. Most elementary students not only love to move, but they actually need to. As a matter of fact, students at this young level will move their bodies frequently whether you want them to or not. Therefore, it makes sense to use movement in the classroom environment with a teacher-directed goal in mind. On limited occasions elementary students will be unmotivated to participate in movement activities. This is against their physical nature at this age. The Kinesthetic Educator will provide an ideal environment for this age group that aligns with the natural instinct of the child. As the unmotivated student engages in movement he or she will quickly develop an appreciation for these activities in the classroom. Hence, discipline problems will decrease, and maximum learning will result.

The secondary student has probably experienced numerous years of learning in a more traditional environment where movement was not utilized in the teaching and learning process. Hence, initially it may not be uncommon to have students show some resistance toward movement.

Many students have created a link between movement and sitting in a seat to learn academic content. A Kinesthetic Educator may be asking a student to participate in academic movement activities that they have never been exposed to in their previous learning years. Some students will respond eagerly as they embrace the change of pace and give the brain the novelty it seeks. Others may shy away from the unknown. They may also link movement in the classroom to movement in the gymnasium, even though they are completely different. These factors may lead to an unmotivated student who simply needs convincing, along with positive experiences involving movement with an academic purpose. This age group has already developed their feelings about living an active or sedentary lifestyle. If a student is active, he or she will be more drawn to a kinesthetic environment. Conversely, if a student is sedentary, he or she may not be interested in moving to learn. However, these students probably need the kinesthetic environment to boost their physical health, which in turn can improve their academic achievement.

Whether you teach elementary school, high school, or anything in between, an unmotivated student can put a significant damper on movement activities in an academic setting. Getting students on board, or reacting effectively when they are not, can be the ultimate test for success or failure in your kinesthetic environment. Allow your excitement and belief in movement to be in the forefront as you consider all strategies and methods to prevent and address these challenges. Be prepared for a trial-and-error process that will build your professional demeanor as you continually improve your management techniques. You will improve as your experiences grow. Your proactive strategies will minimize many situations, and your reactions will become swift, smooth, and consistent. Listed here are several points to consider for managing the unmotivated student in both the elementary or secondary classrooms.

1. Avoid power struggles.
   o Set clear expectations and consequences.
   o Consequences should be fair and effective.
   o Have an alternative activity for students who refuse to participate.
   o Use contracts when necessary.
   o Consider giving a movement grade and incorporate scoring rubrics.

2. Use rewards carefully.
   o Allow movement to be the reward.
   o Movement has an intrinsic motivator because students will feel good.
   o Movement has an extrinsic motivator when students work with their peers in a fun setting.
   o Allow students to choose movements when appropriate to take ownership.

3. Provide security.
   o Show your own value for movement.
   o Prove the benefits to your students.
   o Participate whenever you can.
   o Explain that failure is sometimes a part of learning.
   o Use win-win activities frequently.

4. Build on individual strengths.
   o Allow students to excel and feel success.
   o Build self-esteem with positive feedback.
   o Identify students' interests and incorporate them.
   o Encourage positive peer interactions.
   o Discuss class cohesion benefits.

5. Take ownership.
   o Allow students to create movement activities.
   o Involve students in building the kinesthetic environment.
   o Have students take part in creating rules and consequences.
   o Give movement choices when appropriate.

6. Set and keep expectations high.
   o Expect everyone to participate.
   o Demand all rules and directions are followed accurately.
   o Support the phenomenon of controlled movement with purpose with no exceptions.
   o React to all off-task behavior quickly and consistently.

7. Encourage cooperation.
   o Encourage high fives, fist bumps, and peer compliments.
   o Use activities frequently that promote a team approach.
   o Prohibit put-downs and negative talk.
   o Allow students opportunities to connect with everyone.

Students lacking motivation still want to succeed. Discovering the obstacles that students face will help diminish them over time. With patience, understanding, hard work, and knowledge, you can help all students find a path to achievement and an appreciation for movement. Unmotivated students who refuse to participate will quickly realize the fun that they are missing. Movement in a classroom setting leads to laughter, fun, and learning. These characteristics will eventually win over even the most difficult students. In time, the unmotivated student will learn to see the benefits of learning though movement and begin to look forward to each experience.

Preparing and Reacting to the Hypermotivated Student

The hypermotivated student can be easily found in an elementary setting. It is not uncommon for the educator to manage these behaviors on a daily basis. Developing a kinesthetic learning environment is exactly what these students need. The physical activity will provide them the opportunity to expel any pent-up energy they possess, hence, allowing for more effective seatwork time and attention. These students need movement, and asking them to sit for long periods is an unrealistic request. Oftentimes, when they act out, they are looking for a quick means for releasing this energy. Encouraging hypermotivated students in organized movement activities allows these children the chance to do something their brains and bodies desire.

The hypermotivated student is not as common in a secondary classroom setting; however, these students do exist. As students mature, many become lethargic and inactive in today's society. However, consider the students who are active movers with larger bodies moving in smaller spaces. These situations could become serious concerns if not managed appropriately. Safety will become the only focus in these circumstances, and precise responses will be critical for class control.

Many strategies can be used to manage the hypermotivated student during movement activities in a classroom. The safety of all students is equally important in both an elementary and secondary setting and is always the number one focus. Students who are hypermotivated can quickly lose control of their actions and become a danger to others. These students will require more visual attention. Their actions can be intimidating to others and become a complete distraction to the lesson objectives. Responding to these students quickly and appropriately will keep the situation from escalating and destroying the movement experience for everyone. Diligence is a key component when managing the hypermotivated student during physical movement. Listed here are several points to consider for managing the hypermotivated student in both the elementary or secondary classrooms.

1. Introduce materials observantly.
   - Make sure students hear and understand the directions given.
   - Keep directions precise and clear, and use proximity.

2. Repeat directions.
   - Ask students to repeat directions.
   - Check for understanding before beginning.

3. State clear consequences.
   - Make sure students know the off-task behaviors and the consequences to follow.
   - Review expectations.

4. Respond immediately.
   - Use the consequence that was previously stated.
   - Don't let the little things slide.

5. Be fair and consistent.
   - Explain safety reasons for the consequence.
   - Follow through without hesitation.

6. Avoid power struggles.
   - Keep your voice level down, and do not argue with the student.
   - Restate rules and give consequences.

7. Avoid giving attention.
   - React immediately and appropriately, and move on.
   - Remove student while drawing minimal attention (time-outs can vary in time and send a clear message).

8. Provide feedback.
   - Discuss behavior at opportune times.
   - Ask students why they received a consequence.

9. Set goals.
   - Use short- and long-term goals for behavioral changes.
   - Discuss ideas for behavior control.

Striving for controlled movement with purpose is a reasonable, attainable goal that will yield success. The unmotivated and hypermotivated student will strengthen and define you in many ways. As a Kinesthetic Educator, experiment with your rules, directions, procedures, and consequences to fine-tune your methods. Use each movement lesson as a learning experience for you and your students as you allow the activities to meet everyone's needs. Embrace the feeling as students' motivation grows as they look forward to entering your room while wondering what excitement movement will bring. Imagine your students leaving your room, chatting about your class in the hallway, already excited for tomorrow. The classroom management challenges that movement may initially bring will be well worth your efforts as you master your strategies and techniques. The final result will be a cohesive classroom filled with energy and minimal discipline problems. Movement will become your greatest management tool.

BUILDING AND MANAGING: HOW CAN I TAKE IT TO THE NEXT LEVEL?

Lesson Plans

Should movement activities be written into my lesson plans? This is an intriguing consideration as you define what it means to be a Kinesthetic Educator. As you first begin experimenting with the benefits of movement and its effects on academics, you may not deem it necessary. However, once you are convinced of its value, and you take the true position of becoming a full-time Kinesthetic Educator, you will realize this is the direction you must go. Writing movement objectives into daily lesson plans shows their worth and significance. This is not a difficult or time-consuming task. What follows are a few suggestions for movement objectives.

1. Students will work cooperatively with a partner while actively participating in finger seize and rock-paper-scissors grab during class today. (brain breaks and boosts)

2. Students will actively participate in balloon tap during today's class while respecting individual differences. (class cohesions)

3. Students will actively engage in cross-laterals, criss-crosses, and head, shoulders, knees, and toes (cross and uncross) prior to writing their short stories. (preparing the brain)

4. Students will work cooperatively in groups while actively participating in a volleyball review to prepare for tomorrow's unit test. (reviewing content)

5. Students will learn cardinal directions by physically demonstrating them as they hear them read aloud in a story.

Ideally, the Kinesthetic Educator will use movement whenever possible to review or teach content. This is the ideal use of movement activities in an academic environment. However, in circumstances where a teacher in unable to align movement with the content, activities from "Set" can be used to prepare students for learning, refocus their attention, and increase alertness. In all situations, it is appropriate to add these movements to the lesson by creating reachable standards. If a teacher fails to add movement activities directly into the lesson plan, he or she often forgets to use them. Also, if a teacher does not add movement goals to the lesson, he or she may end up using the same activities over and over because they are the first ones to come to mind when he or she sees students drifting. Take the extra step, and add movement objectives into every lesson plan and each class you teach. This shows a strong commitment to your beliefs in movement and its effectiveness in improving academic achievement. A daily habit of writing the objective will become a daily routine of implementing it.

Movement Makes the Grade

Should students receive a grade for movement in my classroom? There is no right or wrong answer to this question. Schools and teachers have various beliefs about participation grades and what should be included in them. Can you be a successful Kinesthetic Educator without giving a grade for movement? In many instances you can engage students in movement activities simply because they are fun. As a result, many educators may feel that movement activities act as a reward and receiving a grade is not necessary. However, could giving a grade for participating in movement serve as motivation for a student who is typically not interested in participating in physical activities?

Once you begin to use movement to review and teach content, it becomes very important that all students are engaged in these activities. If a student refuses to participate in a review game, should he or she receive the same grade as the students who contribute to the learning experience for the entire class? What would happen if you gave a study guide in place of a movement activity, and everyone turned it in completed with the exception of an unmotivated student? What would the consequence be in this scenario? Would this affect their grade? Again, there is no clear answer here. However, if you use movement daily in your classroom, allowing students to earn a grade can be a great motivator for select, unmotivated students. Additionally, a good grade would be a positive reward for eager participants who always try their best. It is definitely a consideration for the full-time Kinesthetic Educator who is trying to produce an optimal environment where teaching and learning though movement become conventional.

CHAPTER SUMMARY

- Using kinesthetic teaching methodologies in your classroom is about both you and your students exploring and experiencing positive feelings about movement where academic achievements are increased, social connections are made, and everyone feels good about themselves.
- Your primary responsibility as a Kinesthetic Educator is to consider the safety of your students prior to moving them in a classroom environment.
- Your delivery to your students about becoming a Kinesthetic Educator is immense. Not only will you be teaching through movement, but they will be learning through movement as they become a kinesthetic classroom.
- Educators should teach and master their classroom routines linked to movement. This includes, but may not be limited to, transitioning from movement to seat, moving desks, and getting in to partners or groups.
- To have successful classroom management in a kinesthetic environment, it is critical to include proactive strategies that may prevent challenges from occurring.
- Effective management of student behaviors during movement activities is a skill that develops as you continue to experiment with various methods.
- The two main concerns regarding classroom management with the kinesthetic classroom are the unmotivated and the hypermotivated student. Preventive strategies must also be considered and executed with these students. However, reacting appropriately to a student

who refuses to follow your directions will build or destroy the kinesthetic environment.

- As the unmotivated student engages in movement, he or she will quickly develop an appreciation for these activities in the classroom. Hence, discipline problems will decrease, and maximum learning will result.
- Many strategies can be used to manage the hypermotivated student during movement activities in a classroom. The safety of all students is equally important in both an elementary and secondary setting and is always the number one focus.
- Striving for controlled movement with purpose is a reasonable, attainable goal that will yield success. The unmotivated and hypermotivated student will strengthen and define you in many ways. As a Kinesthetic Educator, experiment with your rules, directions, procedures, and consequences to fine-tune your methods.
- Writing movement objectives into daily lesson plans shows their worth and significance.
- Giving a grade for movement is a consideration for the full-time Kinesthetic Educator who is trying to produce an optimal environment where teaching and learning though movement become conventional.

TIPS FOR THE STAFF DEVELOPER

We are often questioned about movement and classroom management. Although we cover it in our graduate courses, it is not something we discuss during workshops unless it comes up as a question. As teachers experience a kinesthetic classroom, they naturally feel at ease about management. If you are presenting about the topic of movement to a staff for the first time, you might want to include some highlights of this chapter in your presentation.

5

Creating Cohesion

➪ Does the emotional climate in my classroom affect student learning?

➪ How often should I use class cohesion activities in my classroom?

➪ What are five activities I can use at the beginning of the year to develop class cohesion?

➪ What are four activities that build classroom connections throughout the school year?

➪ Is competition appropriate in my classroom, and what are four activities that build team unity?

DOES THE EMOTIONAL CLIMATE IN MY CLASSROOM AFFECT STUDENT LEARNING?

Have you ever realized halfway through the school year that your students don't even know one another's names? Many students lead very stressful lives and have minimal emotional connection with other students, which can have adverse effects on the way they think and feel. Children are predisposed to feelings of loneliness, and this can escalate during adolescence. Your students are changing cognitively, mentally, emotionally, physically, and socially as they grow and develop, and this can be a difficult and confusing time in their lives (Yarcheski, Mahon, & Yarcheski, 2011). It is not uncommon for students to have limited communication skills, difficulty with making friends, or life experiences that have had devastating results. Hence, these emotional challenges can clearly affect a student's ability to perform at higher levels academically.

As a teacher, can you really influence students' emotional states if they have so much turmoil outside of your classroom? You have more power over a student's state of mind than you may realize. Yes, you may sometimes feel like you are fighting an uphill battle; however, you have the ability to create an atmosphere where students feel safe, comfortable, and happy. These feelings are necessary to increase speed and win the education race. Developing a cohesive environment in your classroom is a powerful means for getting students ready for higher-level thinking. As previously mentioned, the emotional state of a student is more important to the brain than learning new information. Therefore, it is essential to create an environment that fosters positive feelings and connectedness. Some benefits for engaging students in class cohesion activities include the following:

- Providing a brain break or boost
- Improving communication and listening skills
- Providing an opportunity for problem solving and higher-level thinking
- Offering an environment that promotes laughter and fun while engaging learners
- Improving motivation and discipline
- Heightening students' interest in attending and participating in class
- Building relationships and a general concern for one another
- Developing a sense of belonging
- Improving self-esteem

We already know that certain encounters and happenings make us feel good and bring us pleasure. An upbeat song on the radio, a funny TV show, or spending time with special people can lift our spirits instantaneously. Movement used purposefully in an academic setting can have this same result. Students will laugh together, solve problems with a united effort, and operate with an interconnected approach that will result in feelings of acceptance and enjoyment. Moods will heighten, and students will no longer feel lonely and isolated in your kinesthetic classroom environment. These feelings are ideal for readying the brain to improve academic achievement while optimizing critical thinking and rigorous content.

As a Kinesthetic Educator it is important for you to understand the benefits and importance of developing cohesion in your classroom as it essential to winning the race and optimizing student performance. These activities will help students feel accepted, respected, and connected in your environment, and as a result their brains will be ready for peak learning and achievement. Students will enter your classroom with smiles on their faces as they are excited to learn new information with feelings of comfort and delight with the new friends they have made. Ultimately, this atmosphere will enable them to leave their problems at the door as they dive into becoming active learners participating in activities that require their full attention while providing an escape from life's personal challenges. Additionally, this will allow your academic content to be their sole focus and an optimistic constant in their lives.

Moreover, students will learn the valuable lesson of how to collaborate with peers with whom they may have difficulty connecting. In life, we are often faced with circumstances where we have to get along with someone whose personality clashes with ours. This is an essential life skill that students are losing as a result of technology and social media. A kinesthetic environment can develop this skill while teaching students the importance of teamwork, patience, and respect for individual differences. The movement activities used in your environment will show students how to collaborate even in situations where thoughts and ideas are being pulled in different directions. This is the epitome of higher-level thinking and problem solving.

HOW OFTEN SHOULD I USE CLASS COHESION ACTIVITIES IN MY CLASSROOM?

While being held accountable for today's vigorous curricula, many teachers feel overwhelmed with the idea of making time to focus on class cohesion as yet another responsibility. However, creating a comfortable, interconnected environment is beneficial and crucial to the learning process. Yes, these activities take time to implement in the classroom, but their value is immeasurable. Initially, it may appear as though time is being taken away from academic content. However, the end result is that a cohesive class works quicker and more efficiently through academic challenges as the year proceeds. It is essential to understand the exact role of these interactive movements. Class cohesion activities are not intended for daily use. Therefore, the choice of when the most appropriate times throughout the year to engage students in these activities is critical. The beginning of the school year is an optimal time to incorporate class cohesion activities. This provides students with the opportunity to get to know one another's names, strengths, and personalities. Creating a friendly and comfortable classroom environment from the first day of school is important to the level of success experienced. It is the educator's responsibility to provide these opportunities for students to call one another by name while participating in activities that require and build teamwork. Aside from the beginning of the school year, here are some suggested times to include students in class cohesion activities:

- Right after a big test or the following day
- The day before or the day after a break in the school calendar (holidays)
- When students are not connecting with one another
- During standardized tests
- After a tragic event in the school or community
- The beginning of a new semester
- After rearranging seats in a classroom

WHAT ARE FIVE ACTIVITIES I CAN USE AT THE BEGINNING OF THE YEAR TO DEVELOP CLASS COHESION?

As stated, the prime time to build class cohesion is at the very beginning of the school year or when you first meet your new class. This is typically a time when students feel awkward and uncomfortable around their peers. Providing opportunities for students to learn about one another can help to overcome feelings of angst, fear, or worry. This can be a difficult obstacle depending on your class makeup. Nonetheless, this is a challenge that the Kinesthetic Educator must face to get students ready for a year or semester of high performance and academic success. Moreover, these activities will also provide the educator with equal opportunities to make connections with their students. Developing a bond with your students is often one of the most crucial pieces in motivating them to participate and perform productively in your class while exceeding expectations. An appropriate focus for class cohesion activities at the beginning of the year or semester is to concentrate on learning one another's names. Addressing peers and students by name initiates personal connections that build comfort, trust, and comradeship. Here are four activities that will tackle this challenge.

1. Name Switch on the Move
    - Students will right their name on a piece of paper while adding a sign or symbol that describes something about them.
    - Students will then stand up and mill around the room while politely greeting every student they pass.
    - Greetings will consist of comments such as, "Good morning," "Nice to see you," and "How are you today?" (Encourage eye contact and manners while students mill around.)
    - Every time a student greets another student, he or she also switches name tags. Name tags will be switched numerous times until a teacher says, "Freeze and find your friend."

o At this time, each student will read the name on his or her card while scanning the room to find this person. They will go up to the person they believe is on the name tag they currently have to confirm that they have the right person.

o They may say something like "Hi, are you Bob? I notice you had a football on your name tag; do you play on a team?"

o If a student does not know who the person is on the name tag, he or she can ask others for help.

o The teacher will then instruct the class to start to mill around while continually passing name tags until instructed to freeze once again.

o The length of the game is up to the discretion of the teacher, but the goal is for students to learn as many names as possible.

2. Scatter

o Organize the class into groups of five or six on a team.

o Ask each group to make an original pattern while tossing a ball or object in a small circle to the same person every time and receiving it from the same person consistently.

o After ample repetition, instruct groups to practice their reverse pattern, which will be the same pattern in the opposite order.

o After groups know both patterns fluently, the teacher asks the students to scatter; this refers to leaving the group while independently moving around the room with no particular goal in mind.

o The teacher will then say "freeze" and either "original pattern" or "reverse pattern." At this time students are completely spread around the room and must carefully throw the objects around the room while using the correct pattern called by the teacher. (Students stay where they are; they do not come back to their small circle.)

o The most important aspect of this part of the game is safe throws with very soft objects. (Students can move slightly to create a safer throwing path; objects can also be rolled on the floor.)

o After practicing the throwing pattern for a minute or two, the teacher will again ask the students to scatter around the room.

o When the teacher asks the students to freeze again, they will be spread out in different places once more, which may cause some hesitation to remember the original or reverse patterns from the initial small circle they started with.

o A challenge version of this game is to see which group can complete the pattern requested by the teacher the fastest. The group that gets the ball through their pattern the quickest and lifts the ball high in the air wins the round.

o Play multiple rounds to allow students to increase speed and efficiency.

3. Square Dance
   ○ Ask students to write a list of five things that are important to them.
   ○ Under each idea, students will list supporting reasons why it is important to them.
   ○ Then create two circles, one inside the other (or two lines if space is tight).
   ○ Have participants on the inside circle match up with a participant from the outside circle.
   ○ Introduce some basic square dance moves for fun, and allow the students to practice them.

   Square Dance Calls
   a. Circle (left/right)—inner and outer groups move in opposite directions
   b. Swing your partner—with elbows linked students spin one and a half turns so they switch which circle they are in
   c. Do-si-do—back-to back, partners circle one another while switching which circle they are in
   d. Bow to your partner/corner—self-explanatory
   e. Promenade—circles move in the same direction

   ○ Then, instruct the group on the inside of the circle to start a conversation by telling their partners about something that is important to them and why.
   ○ It is the responsibility of the person on the outside to continue the conversation while adding their thoughts and opinions. Discuss the importance of good discussion techniques (eye contact, respectful listening, open-minded listening, etc.).
   ○ Allow for a two- to three-minute discussion.
   ○ Then have students practice some more square dance moves again.
   ○ After a few minutes, allow participants to match up with a new partner, while the inner person starts the conversation again. (The inner circle should always be changing as they do-si-do and swing their partners.)
   ○ Continue for a few rounds of discussion with square dance practice moves in between each round.

4. Tap and Move
   ○ Put students in four equal teams, and ask them to make a small circle.
   ○ Give each student a balloon or beach ball (a balloon is easier because it has longer air time).
   ○ A student will call someone's name in the circle while tapping the balloon to them.

- After he or she taps the balloon, he or she moves around the outside of the circle to stand behind the student whose name he or she just called.
- The student whose name was called will then call a new name, tap the balloon to that person, and move around the outside of the circle to go stand behind the newly called student.
- The game continues until the balloon is dropped or the circle is no longer recognizable; then a new round begins.
- Eventually, the teacher can join two small groups together to increase the challenge.
- With advanced groups, the teacher can also add more balloons and continue to increase the size of the circle, all while learning more names.

5. Roll Call
   - Split the class into two or four equal teams (the rules are the same either way).
   - Have each team huddle for 30 seconds to decide which team member will step forward for roll call.
   - After teams have made their decisions, the teacher will ask the teams to form their lines. (Decisions are not shared at this time.)
   - When the teacher says, "Roll call," the student who was previously chosen by his or her team now steps forward.
   - The first team to say the name of the person who stepped forward wins that round, and that person joins the winning team.
   - Teams will rehuddle to choose their next person for roll call.
   - If four teams are playing, the teacher may need a helper to listen for winning teams.

WHAT ARE FOUR ACTIVITIES THAT BUILD CLASSROOM CONNECTIONS THROUGHOUT THE SCHOOL YEAR?

Beginning your school year or semester with movement activities to learn names and build relationships is an ideal start for forming bonds that will ensure higher academic goals being set and reached. Students will learn from one another as they grow cognitively and interpersonally. Having a high level of personal comfort in your classroom will allow for optimal learning connections for students and teacher alike. Some students will find themselves in leadership roles, while others will be choosing which candidates to follow. These responsibilities are a part of life and help build character. It is sometimes thought that being a good leader is the most important position one could take regarding a team approach toward meeting a challenge. However, making an intelligent decision about who is a good leader to follow is equally important. Throughout the year, the Kinesthetic Educator will look for opportune times to foster these roles while building a cohesive environment where laughter is present and positive relationships are formed. What follows are four cohesion activities that can be used throughout the school year that will allow classroom dynamics to flourish and take shape.

1. Duck and Point
   o Participants form a circle with the teacher standing in the center.
   o The teacher spins around (slowly) and eventually stops and points at a student and says, "Duck."
   o That person ducks down to the ground.
   o The people on the right and left of the person who ducked have to race to point at one another.
   o The person who points the fastest wins that round and takes the teacher's place in the center of the circle. (The game can also be played where the person who loses is out for one or two rounds and later reenters the game.)
   o Continue by playing as many rounds as time allows.
   o This can also easily be turned into a name game.

2. Human Trouble
   o Make small "Trouble" games around the room by using 16 floor spots per each game.
   o Ten floor spots will be in a circle. Three will go up the middle on one side of the board to represent one team's home scoring, while the three remaining will go up the middle of the other side for the other team's scoring base (16 spots total).
   o Make teams of two to four.
   o On one board game, you will have one team of three versus another team of three, for example.
   o Give each student his or her own die and have groups determine the order of who will go first, second, third, and so on.
   o All participants start the game outside the circle by their home base.
   o A player must roll a 1 or 5 to come into the game on the first spot.
   o He or she will then get a second roll.
   o Students will move the number of spots based on the roll of the die.
   o The game continues as each person takes his or her turn.
   o If the student rolls the die and ends on a spot that is already occupied, that person must go home and start over by trying to roll a 1 or 5 to get back in the game.
   o This is a timed game. Play for 10 to 15 minutes. If someone gets around the board (10 spots) and back into home (three spots), that student wins. This person can play again by starting over and trying to roll a 1 or a 5.

- A player earns a point for the team every time he or she gets completely around the board.
- At the end of the game, the team with the most points wins.
- How many games you set up around the room will be determined by the size of your class.
- You can adjust the game to have four teams of two to four students on one board game.
- Consider turning this cohesion activity into a review game, similar to that of *Jeopardy.*

3. Dragon Tail or Peacock
   - Set boundaries for this walking game.
   - Give everyone a scarf to tuck in the back of his or her pants as a tail.
   - Each student will try to snatch other players' tails while continually trying to protect his or her own.
   - Players cannot protect their tails by using their hands.
   - If a student steals someone's tail, he or she now has two and tucks it in his or her pants and continues to play.
   - Players can only steal one tail at a time.
   - If more than one tail is accidentally taken, extras must be returned.
   - If a player does not have a tail, he or she is still in the game as the student can still steal one from any player who has one.
   - Players with the most tails at the end of the game are the winners.
   - While participants are adding new tails to their collection, they are temporarily out of the game for a few seconds until they are ready for play.
   - After a few rounds of this version, have students get a partner (only one tail is needed).
   - The front player will be the driver and stealer of the tails.
   - The second player gets behind the driver and puts his or her hands on the partner's shoulders.
   - The second player is the protector of the tail (and not allowed to use his or her hands to protect it)
   - Teams must stay connected and work together by following the same rules as the previous game.
   - Teams may also increase in numbers with more advanced groups.

4. Masquerade
   - Have students mill around the room by themselves.
   - Call out a person, place, thing, or idea you would like the students to become (e.g., a skyscraper, tree, mouse, dolphin, creative writer, car, etc.).
   - Have students mill around the room between each round while using eye contact, manners, and kind greetings.
   - Play for a few rounds, and then add partners. "Join a friend and become . . ." (a bridge, ocean, flower, chair, etc.).

- ○ After a few rounds, have students work in groups of three. "Join two friends and become . . ." (a firework celebration, zoo, debate, family of ducks, etc.).
- ○ Always have students mill between rounds to ensure various group dynamics.

IS COMPETITION APPROPRIATE IN MY CLASSROOM, AND WHAT ARE FOUR ACTIVITIES THAT BUILD TEAM UNITY?

Competition in an academic setting refers to student/partners versus student/partners scenarios or a team-against-team approach with a goal of creating group unison. Opinions differ about the role that competition serves concerning movement activities in a classroom environment. Some individuals hold strong beliefs that competition is not necessary and should be avoided at all costs. The philosophy contained in this book will support the idea of a balance between competitive and noncompetitive activities. Allowing students to compete in certain situations is simply a part of life. Every student must learn the concept of winning graciously as well as losing respectfully. Children and adolescents are often rewarded for participating in events or activities despite their success throughout the process. This is appropriate at times because effort is often the most important contribution. However, this may also raise some level of concern. Are children able to lose or fail at something while maintaining their composure? It appears that many children and adolescents handle this sense of failure with anger, sadness, and disgust.

Many individuals are drawn to, or motivated by, competition. When implementing class cohesion activities, whether they're perceived as competitive or not, the most important aspect is presentation. Competition is meant to be positive. Learning how to cheer for and support teammates demonstrates kindness. Being confident to share a compliment with the opposing team shows pride and respect. Promoting an environment where everyone is a winner, even if the game is lost, teaches value and sportsmanship. Many life lessons can be taught during competitive events.

Class cohesion activities will build unity when individuals, partners, or teams challenge one another in given events that work effectively in a classroom setting. This form of competition shapes independent strength or togetherness as individuals and teams must form strategies and demonstrate a succinct effort to accomplish a task. The implementation of these activities will cause excitement among students. Promoting consideration toward teammates and/or opposing team members will be the focus for everyone. These activities are fun, energizing, and engaging for all students.

Class cohesion activities that promote team unity will additionally help the Kinesthetic Educator build an interconnected classroom environment where students feel accepted. Students will need to support one another, follow the rules, and actively participate for the game and/or activity to succeed. Students will love to compete to win as these activities may even excite students who are typically unmotivated during your class. Here are four movement activities that can be used to build cohesion and team unity.

1. Table Hockey
   ○ Have students get in a team of four; with a game strategy of two against two. (A player is able to play by him- or herself in situations where there are an odd number of players; therefore, it will be two against one.)
   ○ Give each group a total of three pennies.
   ○ This is a tag team event; player 1 and 2 go against player 3 and 4.
   ○ Once player 1 goes against player 3 and vice versa, they tag out and player 2 competes with player 4.
   ○ Player 1 goes first against player 3.
   ○ Player 3 makes a goal by spreading his or her index and pinky fingers while placing his or her knuckles against the table across from player 1.
   ○ Player 1 gets a "break" followed by three shots or fewer (after the break) to score a goal. A break is two pennies against one another (lying flat on the table), directly in front of player 1. While placing the index finger on the back penny (a third penny), player 1 slides the penny backward, then forwards to hit the two pennies in the front (similar to a break in the game of pool).
   ○ Now, player 1 has three moves or fewer to score into player 3's goal.
   ○ Rules for moves are as follows: the penny being pushed by the index finger must always go between the other two pennies, the player pushes and releases the penny with the index finger. If any pennies go off the table or touch one another, the turn is over. A goal is scored if a penny goes between the index finger and pinky.
   ○ After player 1 takes a turn, he or she makes a goal with his or her pinky and index fingers, and player 3 follows the same rules. (During the game between player 1 and player 3, player 2 observes and helps player 1, while player 4 helps player 3.)
   ○ After player 3's turn is completed, a tag is made, and players 2 and 4 enter the game to follow the same rules.

2. Scramble
   ○ Break the class into teams of four.
   ○ Word Scramble: Give each team member a letter on a large piece of paper (for example, S, P, O, and T).
   ○ Each team will have the exact same letters.
   ○ At this point, the teacher will read a word and say, "Go."

- The first team that spells that word for the teacher to be able to read it correctly wins.
- Any team that starts before the word "go" automatically loses the game. Below are some sample words to read:
  a. Post
  b. Tops
  c. Pots
  d. Stop
  e. Spot
- Number Scramble: Give each team member a number on a large piece of paper (e.g., 1, 2, 3, 4, and 5).
- Follow the same directions as Word Scramble.

3. Scarf Tag
   - Split the class into three even teams.
   - Give each team a colored scarf, for example, a pink, green, and yellow team.
   - Each team member's job is to tag anyone from another team with a free hand and say, "Frozen" (the other hand holds the scarf).
   - If a person gets tagged, he or she squats to the floor and is frozen.
   - If someone on a team (with the same-colored scarf) switches scarves with the frozen player and says, "Rescue," he or she is unfrozen and back in the game.
   - Students can only unfreeze their own teammates.
   - Every two minutes or less, the teacher stops the game. The team that has the most people unfrozen gets a point.
   - Play multiple rounds.

4. Penny Drop
   - Split the class into two teams.
   - One team will start the game against one wall, and the opposing team will be across from them on the other wall.
   - On each side of the room, there are five small cups spread out, each containing 10 pennies.
   - Therefore, each team has 50 cents.
   - Each team's money is held in the cups on the other side of the room.
   - The ultimate goal is to be the team with the most money after a three- to five-minute game.
   - Team members will take a penny out of one of the cups on their side of the room.
   - They will try to go across the room to deposit the penny into one of their cups on the other side of the room.
   - Although they can only take one penny out of the other team's cup at a time, they can also "steal" a penny from the other team by tagging them as they pass them by (no tag backs).

- Players can tag as many people as they want as they cross the room, which will allow them to deposit many pennies in their cups on the other side.
- Players can lose the pennies they carry at any time.
- They are only safe when they drop the pennies into their cups.
- If someone doesn't have a penny, or has just deposited them, he or she can get another one by tagging someone on the other team who has one or by going back to the side where he or she started the game and taking a penny from the other team's cup.
- After a few minutes, the teacher stops the game, the pennies are counted, and a winner is announced.
- Play a few rounds when time allows.

Creating cohesion in your classroom is an important step in getting students ready for peak learning and performance. A Kinesthetic Educator will become efficient at initiating a unified approach with movement at the beginning of the school year by using activities to learn names and build connections. This expert will also look for prime opportunities to develop unity throughout the year with noncompetitive as well as competitive activities that result in a respectful, fulfilling environment where students have trust, comfort, and camaraderie. These movement activities will allow students to establish a rapport that holds relationships and learning in high regard while producing elevated achievements and rewards that are both academic and interpersonal in nature. Students will develop a fellowship that flows outside your classroom and bonds our younger generation in a way that is desired by all. Hence, taking the time to develop class cohesion will truly build not only your classroom but the school environment in its entirety.

CHAPTER SUMMARY

- It is not uncommon for students to have limited communication skills, difficulty with making friends, or life experiences that have had devastating results. Hence, these emotional challenges can clearly affect a student's ability to perform at higher levels academically.
- Developing a cohesive environment in your classroom is a powerful means for getting students ready for higher-level thinking.
- Some benefits for engaging students in class cohesion activities include the following: providing a brain break or boost, improving communication and listening skills, providing an opportunity for problem solving and higher-level thinking, offering an environment that promotes laughter and fun, improving motivation and discipline, heightening students' interest, building relationships and a general concern for one another, developing a sense of belonging, and improving self-esteem.

- Aside from the beginning of the school year, here are some suggested times to include students in class cohesion activities: right after a big test or the following day, the day before or the day after a break in the school calendar (holidays), when students are not connecting with one another, during standardized tests, after a tragic event in the school or community, the beginning of a new semester, and after rearranging seats in a classroom.
- Five activities that can be used at the beginning of the year to develop class cohesion are: Name Switch on the Move, Scatter, Square Dance, Tap and Move, and Roll Call.
- Four activities that build classroom connections throughout the year are: Duck and Point, Human Trouble, Dragon Tail, and Masquerade.
- Four activities that build team unity are: Table Hockey, Scramble, Scarf Tag, and Penny Drop.
- Class cohesion activities will allow students to establish a rapport that holds relationships and learning in high regard while producing elevated achievements and rewards that are both academic and interpersonal in nature.

TIPS FOR THE STAFF DEVELOPER

Teachers will naturally have questions about how often to use these types of activities. Although we do provide answers to that question, it also depends on the grade level of the students. Although they are critical at every level, elementary teachers will use cohesion activities more frequently than a middle or high school teacher. When you lead a group in one of these activities, be sure to ask them why it was so effective and useful for the classroom and how it might be a lead-in to another lesson or cooperative grouping.

PART 3

SET

Energizing the Brain

6

Preparing the Brain

⇨ Can specific physical movements stimulate and prepare the brain for learning?

⇨ How should brain-compatible movements be used to prepare the brain for learning?

⇨ How can I link brain-compatible movements to academics?

⇨ How will preparing-the-brain activities be delivered in this book?

⇨ What are preparing-the-brain movement challenges I can use with my students?

CAN SPECIFIC PHYSICAL MOVEMENTS STIMULATE AND PREPARE THE BRAIN FOR LEARNING?

Many theorists conclude that there are specific physical movements, in particular ones that include crossing the midline, spinning, balancing, and jumping, that help prepare the brain for learning while improving brain function and communication. As researchers continue their studies on understanding how children and adolescents learn, there are signals that brain development is enhanced through movement. Preparing the brain for learning incorporates specific brain-compatible movements that improve neural connections. In other words, neurons (brain cells) can communicate more effectively with one another so cognitive abilities are enhanced. Although this research is promising, further studies are needed that include consistent measurements with large experimental groups. Moreover, the philosophy presented in this book supports the notion that these specific movements may stimulate the brain as intended but additionally serve as effective brain breaks and boosts that also support exercise and fitness. Therefore, a win-win approach is established.

One of the goals of a brain-compatible classroom is to establish a brain-friendly learning environment. Some of these characteristics include: establishing safe and supportive surroundings, offering a rich, stimulating atmosphere, providing a community approach, creating opportunities for group learning, allowing the brain to make connections while purposefully using transfer, incorporating rehearsal and practice, working within memory time and capacity limits, and incorporating movements that facilitate cognition. There are specific programs, which have existed for decades, that provide impressive evidence that shows these brain-compatible activities are beneficial and effective in preparing the brain and enhancing the learning process.

Exercises that cross the midline of the body along with movements that stimulate the vestibular system and improve spatial awareness are beneficial for preparing the brain for learning. These activities (spinning, jumping, balancing, and combination challenges) not only are fun but are also intended to open channels in the brain for improved communication. Each hemisphere of the brain controls the opposite side of the body. A thick bundle of 250 million nerve fibers called the corpus callosum connects the two hemispheres and allows them to communicate. Crossing the midline refers to moving the arms and/or legs across the body from one side to the other. These integrative movements help students prepare for learning by forcing the hemispheres to work together, assisting in energy and blood flow, decreasing muscle tension, and stimulating and focusing the brain to improve concentration (Dennison & Dennison, 1988; Hannaford, 1995; Promislow, 1999). The eyes also move in various pathways similar to the limbs (Dennison & Dennison, 1988). This is called visual tracking. Tracking is the ability of the eyes to follow an object. If brain hemispheres are not efficiently communicating with each other, reading and writing can be difficult. Although there is limited technical research on these movements, the logic supporting them is very powerful (Jensen, 2000).

Many children who experience learning disabilities struggle with crossing the midline of the body. These students will often have difficulty with reading and writing (Pica, 2006). By incorporating cross-lateral movements into your classroom regimen, you may help improve these skills. Although there is no guarantee, these activities can't hurt and will probably energize your students (Jensen, 2000). Although humans do not strictly prefer the left or right hemisphere, most people have a dominant side. Cross-lateral activities can help students use both sides of the brain while improving skills they are lacking. Learning how to read and write, thinking clearly, and problem solving are skills that involve both hemispheres of the brain.

The vestibular system provides the brain with meaningful information. This visual system is related to motion or the position of the head and body in space. The vestibular system accomplishes two major tasks. First, it contributes to an individual's sense of equilibrium and conveys information to the muscles and posture. Second, it controls eye movements, so images remain steady and in focus. This explanation helps to rationalize a connection between the vestibular system and academic skills. The vestibular system is most critical for cognition and is the first sensory system to develop (Jensen, 2000). As a result, it serves as an organization tool for other brain processes while playing a key role in perception. Therefore, balance problems can hinder brain function.

Spatial awareness allows us to sense both objects in the space around us and the body's position in space. Without this awareness, students may have difficulty with the following: reading, organizing written work, understanding abstract math concepts, and reproducing patterns and shapes. Studies have suggested a connection between abstract thinking and a well-developed sense of spatial awareness. The developing brain needs to activate this system adequately, so movement and cognitive growth can develop (Jensen, 2000). Various spinning, balancing, jumping, rolling, turning, and combination activities can help develop and improve the vestibular system and spatial awareness. Movements that stimulate the inner ear alert the brain to sensory stimuli (Hannaford, 1995). The more senses that are used for learning, the more likely information will be stored and retrieved from memory.

HOW SHOULD BRAIN-COMPATIBLE MOVEMENTS BE USED TO PREPARE THE BRAIN FOR LEARNING?

Preparing-the-brain movements play an important role in "setting" the brain for improved learning and performance. These activities are appropriate for most grade, fitness, and ability levels and require minimal space. Another considerable benefit of these movements is that they can be implemented in a one- to two-minute time frame throughout your lessons. When deciding how to incorporate them, consider your objective. For example, if you are asking students to read and/or write, it is reasonable to engage students in brain-compatible movement activities that cross the midline of the body. Both hemispheres of the brain are involved with reading and writing. Your goal is to get both sides of the brain communicating to achieve greater success with the presented challenge. Students can also participate in activities that develop the vestibular system to better track words or numbers on a page. These fun, simple movements are easy to incorporate. Look for windows that present an ideal opportunity to pre-pare the brain for learning. Here are a few to consider:

- Prior to standardized tests
- At the start of the day
- Before diving into an academic goal
- Between academic activities
- When students show signs of boredom
- When students appear restless
- Before and during testing
- While teaching and reviewing your academic content

Not only are these activities quick to implement, but no equipment is needed, and classroom management is minimal. These qualities make preparing-the-brain movements ideal to implement near the beginning of the year, when you are first building your confidence and comfort level regarding kinesthetic activities. Of course, they should continue to be used consistently throughout the year during appropriate times to set the brain for peak performance. An additional strength of these short bursts of movement is that they are typically done independently. This aspect makes these activities easier to implement than ones where students are working with partners or small groups. Finally, preparing-the-brain move-ments are perfect activities with multiple strengths and ease of use that promote improved brain communication for superior learning.

HOW CAN I LINK BRAIN-COMPATIBLE MOVEMENTS TO ACADEMICS?

Anchoring content with movement combines academic pursuits and kinesthetic activities, which has been shown to increase test scores in elementary students (Blaydes Madigan & Hess, 2004). Creative thought in the design of these activities will enhance the entire process. Academic content and specific movements can be combined in many ways. For instance, students can do the following:

- Perform heel taps or windmills while reciting the alphabet.
- Juggle one or two scarves while counting odd and even numbers.
- Spin 360 degrees while understanding the planets and the solar system.
- Point to designated places on a map while holding a balance pose.
- Leap frog to the points on a geometric shape.
- Jump rope while reading a word wall.

Allowing children and adolescents to participate in preparing-the-brain movements that facilitate learning should prove beneficial and fun. At the very least, these activities serve to reenergize learners as they pursue academic goals and standards while moving their bodies. Therefore, it only makes sense to combine these movements with academics whenever possible.

HOW WILL PREPARING-THE-BRAIN ACTIVITIES BE DELIVERED IN THIS BOOK?

There are many ways to use preparing-the-brain activities to set the stage for enhanced learning. In this book we will focus on movement challenges that will not only heighten brain communication as is intended but also provide an energy that naturally motivates the participant. Innately, we are driven by challenges that we set for ourselves or ones that are given to us by others. These tests drive us due to our instinct to avoid failure and experience success. These pleasurable feelings are rewarding, desired, and push us to our limits in an effort to experience the gratification of triumph.

The movement challenges contained herein will include the following: 60 in 60 Cross, Spin 30, 30–60 Hold, 30 in 30 Jumps, and Partner High 60. The "60" and "30" refer to both time (seconds) and the desired number of repetitions for achievement. Each physical movement can be modified for the various skill levels in your classroom; however, the ultimate goal is to reach or exceed the suggested repetitions in the given time frame. As a result of the time limit, students may increase their participation speed. This will allow for a secondary benefit of supporting exercise and fitness while increasing oxygen, blood flow, and energy. It is neither necessary nor recommended to increase speeds to a point of exhaustion. That is not the intention of preparing-the-brain activities. The purpose of these activities is to improve neural communication, hence speeds can be quickened but not rushed. Keep in mind, fitness is a secondary benefit of these challenges but not the main objective.

WHAT ARE PREPARING-THE-BRAIN MOVEMENT CHALLENGES I CAN USE WITH MY STUDENTS?

There are 25 challenges listed in this section. Encourage students to move at comfortable speeds with a main focus of performing the given skill with proper form and technique. Keep in mind, as always, the number one focus is safety. Consider your space and personality of your students prior to using these movements. Bear in mind your routines, rules, and structures that are already in place, and be sure to follow them without fail or question. Compliment your students with encouraging words and positive feedback. Invite your students to high-five or fist bump two or more peers at the conclusion of each challenge. Finally, remind students of the purpose of preparing-the-brain activities along with their purposed benefits.

60 in 60 Cross—The goal is to complete 60 repetitions in 60 seconds while crossing the body's midline each time.

1. Grapevine
   - This is a lateral movement where students will face forward as they move sideways.
   - Students will take their right foot and step to the right.
   - They will then step with their left foot and cross it over the front of the right.
   - The next step will be the right foot out to the side followed by the left foot crossing behind the right.
   - Continue this pattern of step, cross in front, step, cross behind, step, cross in front, and so on.
   - In this challenge, do four grapevines to the right, four to the left, and continue (perform two and two in smaller spaces).
   - Modification: Use a slower speed and follow a partner.

2. Windmills
   - Have students stand with their feet wide apart and their arms reaching out to the sides.
   - Students will swing their right hands down to touch their left toes or ankles (straight legs or a slight bend in the knees is appropriate).
   - Stand up and swing the left hand down to the right toes or ankle.
   - Continue at a comfortable speed.
   - Modification: Touch shin or knee.

3. Hand Clapping—Toe Tapping
   - Have students stand with feet shoulder width apart and arms reaching out to their sides.
   - Cross the right foot in front of the left leg, and tap the toe to the ground. At the same time, cross the right arm over the body, and clap with the left hand.
   - Go back to the beginning position.
   - Now, cross the left foot in front of the right leg, and tap the toe to the ground. At the same time, cross the left arm over the body, and clap with the right hand.
   - Go back to the beginning position and continue the pattern.
   - Modification: Use a slower speed and follow a partner.

4. Criss-Crosses
   - Stand with feet shoulder width apart.
   - Jump in the air while simultaneously crossing your left foot in front of your right, then land.

- ○ Jump in the air, uncross your feet, and land.
- ○ Jump, cross your right foot in front of your left, then land.
- ○ Jump and uncross your feet, then land.
- ○ Continue the pattern.
- ○ Modification: Do not jump while crossing feet.

5. Elbow-Knee Touches
   - ○ Cross your right elbow to touch your left knee.
   - ○ Cross your left elbow to touch your right knee.
   - ○ Continue with the pattern.
   - ○ Add a hop while making each cross for higher intensity.
   - ○ Modification: Touch elbow to thigh or as close to the knee as possible.

Spin 30—The goal is to perform as many complete spins as possible in 30 seconds while maintaining safety and balance.

1. One-Legged Hop and Spin
   - ○ Have students bend their knee so the right foot is close to the buttocks.
   - ○ Now with the left hand, they will reach behind their backs and grab the right foot.
   - ○ While hopping on the left foot, they will spin in a clockwise rotation (then counterclockwise).
   - ○ Have students bend the left knee so the left foot is close to the buttocks.
   - ○ Have them reach the right hand behind their backs and grab the left foot.
   - ○ While hopping on the right foot, they will spin in a clockwise rotation (then counterclockwise).
   - ○ Modification: Eliminate the hop.

2. Crab Walk Spin
   - ○ Have students sit on their buttocks on the floor with their knees bent so their feet are flat.
   - ○ Hands are placed on the floor behind their backs with their fingers pointing away from their bodies.
   - ○ Now have students lift their buttocks off the ground so their feet and arms or hands are holding their weight.
   - ○ While keeping their hands in the same area, their feet will rotate in a circular, clockwise position around the hands (then counterclockwise).
   - ○ Modification: Sit on the floor every quarter of a turn.

3. Jumping Jack Spin
   - ○ Have students start by standing tall with their feet together and their arms down at their sides.

- Have students jump and separate their feet to slightly shoulder width apart while bringing their arms together up in the air.
- Continue with pattern while spinning clockwise (then counterclockwise).
- Modification: Eliminate the jump.

4. 360-Degree Spin
   - Have students stand with their feet shoulder width apart and their arms reaching out to the sides.
   - Using a swing-like motion with their arms, have students jump and spin their hips, legs, and feet in a clockwise rotation.
   - The goal is to spin 360 degrees and land back in the original position.
   - Students will complete one spin in this direction then try counterclockwise.
   - Modification: Take a 180 or quarter turn as needed.

5. Partner Spin
   - Have partners cross arms and join hands.
   - While staying connected, spin in one complete circle.
   - Go the other direction.
   - Modification: Use a slower speed.

30–60 Hold—The goal is to hold a balance pose for either 30 or 60 seconds. Start with a 30-second challenge, then increase the time based on student's skill level.

1. Arabesque
   - Have students stand on the right foot (with a straight leg).
   - Students will lift their left legs backward as far as they can without bending them. This will result in the upper body becoming parallel with the floor.
   - Arms should be reaching out on the sides of the body (like an airplane).
   - Practice on both legs.
   - Modification: Keep lifted leg closer to the ground, or hold a steady object to help with balancing.

2. Tree
   - Have students stand with feet shoulder width apart.
   - Students will place most of their weight on the right leg.
   - They will bend the left leg into the inner thigh of the right leg (with the ankle below the knee for students who are struggling).
   - Students will place their palms together as they lift their arms high in the air.

- Switch legs and try the pose again.
- Modification: Place the bended leg below the knee or by the ankle.

3. Chair Balance
   - Have students sit at the edge of their chairs.
   - Students will wrap their hands around the seat of the chair.
   - Allow students to lift their bodies off the chair and lower to the floor directly in front of the chair.
   - Ask students to straighten their legs while lifting one in the air.
   - Have them hold this position for 15 or 30 seconds and then switch legs.
   - Modification: Keep both feet on the ground.

4. Eagle
   - Have students stand with their feet together and knees slightly bent.
   - Students shift their weight onto the left foot, and cross the right thigh over the left. Then they hook the right foot behind the left foot when possible.
   - Have students cross the left elbow over the right (like hugging yourself), and bring the palms of the hands together.
   - Students hug their legs together and sit back slightly.
   - Then they lift their elbows to shoulder height or as close as possible.
   - Modification: Cross legs as far as possible and connect to the wrist or forearm as opposed to palms.

5. Hand to Knee
   - Stand with feet shoulder width apart.
   - Students lift and bend the right leg in the air until the thigh is parallel to the ground.
   - Then they hold the right leg in the air with one or two hands.
   - Switch to the other side.
   - Modification: Keep the lifted leg closer to the ground, and/or use a steady object to help with balancing.

30 in 30 Jumps—The goal is to perform 30 jumps in 30 seconds. A modification for jumping is to lift onto the toes while never leaving the ground. When jumping, always land softly.

1. Jump Squats
   - Students stand with their feet shoulder width apart or slightly more.
   - Then they bend their knees to touch the floor with their hands while trying to keep their backs as straight as possible.
   - Students spring off the ground while raising their arms straight into the air.

○ They land on their feet, bend down to the ground, and continue.
○ Modification: Only have students bend as low as feasible for their bodies and then up onto the toes.

2. Line Jump
   ○ Have students stand on one side of a line (the line can be imaginary) while facing forward.
   ○ Students keep their feet together as they jump sideways across the line to the other side.
   ○ Then they come back to the original side they started on.
   ○ Students continue going side to side across the line while facing forward.
   ○ Modification: Step side to side over the line.

3. Split Leg Jumps
   ○ Have students start with the right leg forward and left leg behind.
   ○ Students bend their knees slightly.
   ○ They jump in the air and switch their feet so that when they land, the left foot is now forward and the right leg is behind.
   ○ Have students continue to jump and switch while maintaining a slight bend in their knees every time they land.
   ○ Modification: Switch feet without jumping.

4. Pogo
   ○ Have students stand with their feet slightly closer than shoulder width apart.
   ○ Students hold their arms high in the air.
   ○ They bend their knees slightly while springing up and down in the air like they are on pogo sticks.
   ○ Modification: Have students lower their arms and spring onto their toes.

5. Box Jump
   ○ Make a plus sign on the floor (this can be imaginary).
   ○ Have students jump into each quadrant while moving clockwise (there are four quadrants).
   ○ Ask students to change direction.
   ○ Modification: Have students step into each quadrant while slowing the speed.

Partner High 60—The goal is to complete the following combination activities in 60 seconds with a partner while combining the scores to try to get the highest total in the class.

1. Two-Ball Juggling
   ○ Each student will have a partner and two balls.
   ○ Partners stand two to six feet apart depending on space, ball size, and skill level.

- They pass the balls back and forth at the same time while trying not to drop them.
- Each catch made counts as a point.
- Total all successful catches.
- Modification: Use a closer distance, larger balls, or one ball (instead of two).

2. Scissor Kicks—Arm Crosses
   - Have both partners begin by placing their arms high in the air and staggering their feet one in front of the other.
   - Students will jump and switch the positions of their feet while crossing their arms in the air at the same time (right arm in front of left).
   - Then have students switch the positions of their feet once again while their arms cross the other way (left arm in front of right).
   - Allow partners to choose their speed.
   - Total scores—each jump and cross counts for one point.
   - Modification: Switch feet without jumping.

3. Air Jump Passes
   - Have partners stand two to six feet apart depending on space, ball size, and skill level.
   - Students will pass the ball to their partners.
   - The partner will catch the ball in the air and throw it back to his or her partner before he or she lands (catch and throw in the air).
   - Points are awarded when an airborne catch and throw is made.
   - Modification: Catch in the air, land, then jump to throw the ball back.

4. Partner Connect
   - Partners face one another approximately an arm's length apart.
   - At the same time, students will tap both their right hands and right feet in the center space between them.
   - They will then tap their left hands and left feet in the center space between them.
   - Partners both must move at the same speed to keep their taps coordinated with one another.
   - Hands and feet tapped counts as one point.
   - Modification: Decrease the speed of taps.

5. Figure Eights
   - Partners will stand four to eight feet apart depending on space, ball size, and skill level.
   - Both students will stand facing one another with bent knees.
   - The student who holds the ball or object passes the ball through his or her legs, around the right leg, back through the middle, and around the left leg while making a pass to his or her partner (this is known as a figure eight).

○ The partner catches the ball or object, does the figure eight, and passes it back.

○ Each catch after a successful figure eight counts as one point.

○ Modification: Use larger balls or objects, closer partner distance, and/or slower speed.

Having students perform these challenges will maintain the purpose of engaging the brain while improving neural connections. These physical movements will not only invigorate students but also help set the brain for improved performance. Students will enjoy these quick activities as they take a break away from traditional seatwork, while fresh oxygen and blood surge through the body. The challenge aspect of the activities will also motivate students as they strive to meet the set goals along with their peers. Creating a positive environment where students encourage and support one another is an essential aspect of preparing the brain while building your kinesthetic environment.

CHAPTER SUMMARY

- Many theorists conclude that there are specific physical movements, in particular ones that include crossing the midline, spinning, balancing, and jumping, that help prepare the brain for learning while improving brain function and communication.
- One of the goals of a brain-compatible classroom is to establish a brain-friendly learning environment by establishing safe and supportive surroundings, offering a rich, stimulating atmosphere, providing a community approach, creating opportunities for group learning, allowing the brain to make connections while purposefully using transfer, incorporating rehearsal and practice, working within memory time and capacity limits, and incorporating movements that facilitate cognition.
- Exercises that cross the midline of the body along with movements that stimulate the vestibular system and improve spatial awareness are beneficial for preparing the brain for learning.
- The vestibular system is the most critical for cognition and is the first sensory system to develop (Jensen, 2000). As a result, it serves as an organization tool for other brain processes while playing a key role in perception.
- Spatial awareness allows us to sense both objects in the space around us and the body's position in space. Without this awareness, students may have difficulty with the following: reading, organizing written work, understanding abstract math concepts, and reproducing patterns and shapes.

- Preparing-the-brain movements are fun, simple movements that are easy to incorporate. Look for windows that present an ideal opportunity to prepare the brain for learning.
- In this book we focus on movement challenges that will not only heighten brain communication as is intended but also provide an energy that naturally motivates the participant.
- The movement challenges contained herein include the following: 60 in 60 Cross, Spin 30, 30–60 Hold, 30 in 30 Jumps, and Partner High 60. The "60" and "30" refer to both time (seconds) and the desired number of repetitions for achievement.
- These physical movements will not only invigorate students but also help set the brain for improved performance.

TIPS FOR THE STAFF DEVELOPER

Make sure to point out that most preparing-the-brain activities are done individually, which for some students make these more fun and accessible. Also be sure to carefully read through the activities you plan to use, and practice as needed. Some are more complicated than others, and you don't want to be in the middle of a professional development session and not know the activity!

7

Providing Brain Breaks

> ⇨ What is the point of a brain break?
>
> ⇨ Are brain breaks the equivalent of brain blasts, boosts, or energizers?
>
> ⇨ What are 15 brain break activities that can be done in two minutes or less?
>
> ⇨ Can these activities be modified to fit the grade level and physical capability of my students?

WHAT IS THE POINT OF A BRAIN BREAK?

Cognitive science informs us that most information needs to be processed, practiced, and rehearsed in varied ways for long-term storage to take place. If processing opportunities are not present, there is a good chance the information will be lost from overload. In short, our working memory capacities are just that—short! The working memories of children are consistently being overloaded with information. Imagine a large pitcher of water being poured into a Dixie cup—the large pitcher being school information and the Dixie cup being the hippocampus. This scenario happens in classrooms every day. Content requirements and strict time limitations box teachers into feeling like they can spare no moment for breaks! The point of a brain break is exactly that: to give the brain a break. As previously discussed, as far as the brain is concerned, shorter is usually better. Brain breaks provide the perfect opportunity to give students a much-needed break from content and prevent working memory over-load. Teaching in small bursts, allowing for the processing and rehearsal of information, and providing brain breaks are sound classroom practices.

ARE BRAIN BREAKS THE EQUIVALENT OF BRAIN BLASTS, BURSTS, BOOSTS, OR ENERGIZERS?

There are more benefits to using brain breaks, all of which play an essential role in winning the education race and improving student success. Many who use them prefer to call them brain blasts, bursts, boosts, or energizers, and yes, they are exactly that as well! Not only do brain breaks provide for a break in content, but they also create more blood and oxygen flow around the brain and body creating a more energized, engaged, and moti-vated student. These activities can completely change the dynamic of a classroom and add considerable quality time to instruction because of the more effective, engaged, and efficient brain now sitting in front of you. We've all been there in meetings, professional learning, graduate courses, and the like where, according to your bottom and your attention span, a break should have been given hours ago. Imagine a child in this scenario. Over the years we've had so much feedback about how these simple activities, which take less than two minutes, have completely changed the dynamic and energy of a learning environment.

It is imperative to consider when and how to integrate brain breaks into lesson plans. Some brain breaks might be easier to implement than others. Start with activities that best fit you and your students. As you gain confidence in using brain breaks, planning will become less of a con-sideration as you will intuitively know when it is time to use one. If you are concerned that students might be unwilling to try the activities, refer to Chapter 4 (Building and Managing a Kinesthetic Classroom), and be prepared to respond quickly and appropriately to these students.

The brain breaks recommended in this book will take approximately two minutes. This time can be slightly extended when students are engaged in the activities for the first time. As students become familiar with these activities, begin to refer to them by name. A poster listing the brain breaks would be a great addition to the classroom. These activities can help intro-duce movement into your classroom. Allow your creative thoughts to flow as you ultimately add to the list.

WHAT ARE 15 BRAIN BREAKS THAT CAN BE DONE IN TWO MINUTES OR LESS?

1. Bib Duel (for younger students) or Duel (for older students and adults)
   o Have each student get a partner.
   o Give each student a juggling scarf (or something similar).

○ Students will use the scarf to make a bib or put in one side of their pants (older students) and stand back-to-back with their partners.

○ When the teacher says, "Draw," students will spin around to face each other. The first student to grab his or her partner's bib wins the round.

○ Play a few rounds, and then switch partners.

○ You may want to play a few warm-up games face-to-face.

2. Show Your Size

○ Have students move around the room.

○ The teacher will call out one of three sizes, "small," "medium," or "tall."

○ Students will squat to show small, stand normal for medium, and stretch as high as they can for tall.

○ Students keep moving until another size is called.

○ The educator can shake things up by saying different sizes and allowing participants to react (super small, Empire State Building, caveman, etc.).

3. Partner Tennis Ball Challenge

○ Have students get in teams of two.

○ Give each team three tennis balls.

○ Take students through the following individual and partner challenges while playing upbeat, lively music.

Individual
a. Around the head
b. Around the waist
c. Around the knees, then two knees, one knee
d. Head, waist, knees together
e. Figure eights
f. Throw ball up, catch behind you
g. Throw, spin, and catch
h. Two- to three-ball juggling
i. Bounce ball, catch it on your knuckles
j. Any other trick you would like to add

Partner
a. Toss one ball back and forth, then two, then three
b. Figure eight, throw it to partner and back
c. Underhand throws, overhand
d. Throw, bounce, and catch
e. Any other trick you would like to add

4. Noodle Baton

○ Have students move the noodle in a figure eight pattern, simulating a baton.

○ The figure eight can be done in front of the body, out to either side, above the head, or looking down upon it.

5. Noodle Twirl
   - While holding the noodle flat on the palm, try to spin around as many times as possible before it hits the ground.
   - Teacher can blow the whistle to have students change directions to increase the challenge.

6. Noodle Relay
   - Make two even teams.
   - Have the first student in line place the noodle between his or her legs at knee height.
   - Students will race while passing the noodle down the line without letting it hit the floor.
   - If the noodle touches the floor, the team must restart.
   - The first team to pass the noodle between their knees down and back without it touching the floor wins.

7. Noodle Creation
   - Place class into small teams, and give them approximately five minutes to create their own noodle brain breaks that they will teach to the class.
   - Everyone in the class will try the new noodle brain break.

8. Mime Introductions
   - Put students into pairs or partners.
   - Instruct students to tell their partners three things about themselves without speaking; use only charades. Then reverse roles.
   - Each student should confirm what his or her partner was trying to tell him or her.
   - A variation on this would be to demonstrate three things about your school, an idea, a character, and so on.
   - Feel free to have students switch partners several times.

9. Funny Face Introductions
   - Have students break into smaller groups of five or six students.
   - Each member introduces him- or herself by saying his or her name in conjunction with a funny facial expression.
   - The group imitates the expression.
   - Every student in the group should have the opportunity to participate.

10. Stand, Breathe, and Relax
    - Have students stand and relax their arms by their sides.
    - On your lead, ask students to draw a long breath in through the nose.
    - Students hold their breath to the count of three.
    - Breath is then released through the mouth.
    - Remind students to focus on their breath throughout this activity.

○ Use the example of where a baby starts its breath (the stomach) to provide good instruction on where your students should begin breathing.

○ This activity will provide blood flow and relaxation.

○ Repeat for 30 to 60 seconds, longer if necessary.

11. Stand, Squeeze, and Relax

○ Have students stand and relax their arms by their sides.

○ At your lead, students should squeeze both fists for a slow three count, then relax.

○ Repeat five or six times.

○ Next, instruct students not only to squeeze their hands but their arms and shoulders as well—all at the same time.

○ Hold to a three count, and repeat five or six times.

○ This progressive muscle relaxation activity will provide blood flow and relaxation.

12. Stand, Breathe, Squeeze, and Relax

○ This is a combination of the two previous activities.

○ Have students inhale and squeeze gradually at the same time.

○ They should hold their breath and squeeze for a count of three.

○ Gradually release their breath and the tension in their shoulders and arms.

13. Stand in Response

○ Prepare a list of questions that you know your students will be able to answer "yes" to at several points during this brain break. Some examples include these:

   a. Do you like to listen to music?
   b. Have you traveled out of state?
   c. Do you like to swim?
   d. Do you like to exercise?
   e. Do you wear glasses?
   f. Do you have braces?

○ Instruct students to stand for a silent count of four if they can answer yes to the question you've asked.

14. Nose and Ear Grab and Switch

○ Instruct students to grab their noses with one hand and crossover with the other hand to grab the opposite ear.

○ On your signal, students should switch as their hands cross in front of their faces, so the ear hand grabs the nose and the nose hand grabs the ear in the same type of switching motion.

○ Caution: This should be carefully practiced, so you have it mastered before showing students. You can see Mike doing this brain break by searching his name on YouTube and watching the video: "Mike Does a Brain Break" (available at https://www .youtube.com/watch?v+dr4-ZfEOs64).

15. Funny Face/Mean Face Jump
    ○ Students should find a partner and face him or her.
    ○ Instruct students to make a really happy, smiley face at their partners.
    ○ Now instruct students to make a really mean, nasty face at their partners.
    ○ Repeat both sets of instructions (laughter will be heard during both).
    ○ Instruct students to stand back-to-back (they should not be touching).
    ○ Instruct students to jump and twist in the air, so they land facing each other.
    ○ While in the air students should make a decision as to show their funny face or their mean face to their partners upon landing.
    ○ The idea is to match—funny to funny or mean to mean.
    ○ Play as many rounds as necessary to provide a laughter-filled and active break.

CAN THESE ACTIVITIES BE MODIFIED TO FIT THE GRADE LEVEL AND PHYSICAL CAPACITY OF MY STUDENTS?

When reading about or learning any new activity, it is imperative to consider the following student characteristics:

- Age
- Physical Skill
- Maturity Level
- Cognitive Ability

Many activities can be altered to fit students with many different needs and ability levels. Sometimes changes can be small, such as using a larger or smaller ball in the activity. Other adjustments may take more consideration to change rules and directions while maintaining a similar goal. For example, a kindergarten teacher might find that the partner tennis ball challenge is too difficult for this particular age group. These students could just learn the more simple parts of the activity first, with additional skill-related parts of the challenge added later in the year if appropriate.

If your intention is to simplify an activity, you must first reflect on what aspect might make it difficult for your students. Are there too many rules? Are the rules too complex? Are your students lacking the coordination to perform the challenge at hand? There are a number of ways to make an activity easier for younger students or individuals with special needs. Here are some suggestions:

- Use a larger ball or object.
- Use a softer ball or object.
- Choose a ball or object that will not drop to the floor as quickly (such as a beach ball).
- Have students stand closer together.
- Chunk the game into smaller sections.
- Encourage students to take their time (slow things down).
- Demonstrate the activity with more than one group.

When working with older students or individuals who have higher skill levels, it is essential that changes be made to activities to meet these students' needs. To make an activity more challenging, a close examination of the rules and directions are required. Here are some suggestions for making an activity more difficult:

- Use a smaller ball or object.
- Choose a ball or object that is denser and will fall more quickly.
- Increase the number of times a task or trick must be completed.
- Complicate the rules.
- Increase the number of people involved in the task (depends on the brain break).
- Set time limits.

Not all students will take pleasure in every activity in which they participate. Personality types, likes, and dislikes will play roles in a student's enjoyment of an activity. Therefore, it is important to vary the brain breaks. It is human nature to do what makes us comfortable. Many teachers will find specific brain breaks to their liking and will be tempted to use the same ones repeatedly. Branching out and trying new things will keep your students guessing.

CHAPTER SUMMARY

- The primary goals of a brain break (boost, blast, burst, or energizer) are to give the brain a break from academic content and provide more blood and oxygen flow around the brain and body.
- Some secondary benefits can also occur such as laughter, problem solving, and higher-order thinking.
- You will also have created a more efficient, engaged, and energized group of students who are more ready to work, pay attention, and engage with content.

- Consider making a poster for your classroom that lists the brain breaks. When you feel ready, add your ideas to the list.
- There are 15 brain breaks contained in this chapter that the educator can implement into his or her lessons in two minutes or less: (1) bib duel, (2) show your size, (3) partner tennis ball challenge, (4) noodle baton, (5) noodle twirl, (6) noodle relay, (7) noodle creation, (8) mime introductions, (9) funny face introductions, (10) stand, breathe, and relax, (11) stand, squeeze, and relax, (12) stand, breathe, squeeze, and relax (13) stand in response, (14) nose and ear grab and switch, and (15) funny face/mean face jump.
- It is important to consider student age, physical skill, maturity level, and cognitive ability when assessing a new activity.
- Simplify activities by using a larger ball or object, choosing a ball or object that will not drop to the floor as quickly, allowing students to stand closer together, chunking games into smaller sections, encouraging students to take their time, and demonstrating the activity with more than one group.
- Make activities more challenging by using a smaller ball or object, choosing a ball or object that is more dense and will fall more quickly, increasing the number of times a task or trick must be completed, complicating the rules, increasing or decreasing the number of people involved in the task (depending on the brain break), and setting time limits.
- Keep it fresh, and vary the brain breaks you use!

TIPS FOR THE STAFF DEVELOPER

Brain breaks are a must for every professional development session or meeting that lasts longer than 30 minutes. Remind participants that they are getting an opportunity to "sit in the seats" of students and getting to feel what it's like to sit for long periods of time. Also remind them that the more they are engaged in the activity, the more likely it is they will remember it.

8

Supporting Exercise and Fitness

> ⇨ Do exercise and fitness belong in a classroom setting, and what is Max 60?
>
> ⇨ What are some basic elements of movement that can be used effectively in a classroom environment with Max 60?
>
> ⇨ What are the Max 60 challenges I can implement in my classroom in two minutes or less?
>
> ⇨ How can exercise and fitness be supported in my classroom if I am not currently active in my own life?

DO EXERCISE AND FITNESS BELONG IN A CLASSROOM SETTING, AND WHAT IS MAX 60?

Absolutely! The decline in the fitness levels of our youth has become such a serious concern that it can no longer be ignored. This younger generation has become obsessed with technology, which usually requires a seated position that is inactive and lethargic. In most case scenarios, students sit all day in school, and then they do the same thing at home. This severe level of inactivity is wreaking havoc on the body and brain and stifling our inner mentality to be physically active human beings. These newly formed

111

habits are resulting in sedentary lifestyles that are defining a new society—unfortunately, one that could lead to the demise of our physical health.

Ideally, we would attack this problem in schools, at home, and through community events and involvement. However, as previously explained, the one place we have the best ability to make the greatest impact is in our educational environment. Here, we can set standards for a new type of teaching and learning process, one that will have students moving throughout the entire day while raising the academic bar. Doesn't that sound ideal? We can improve our children's health and academic achievement both at the same time. By being a Kinesthetic Educator and supporting exercise and fitness in the classroom, we can do just that. The rewards will be twofold and will breed a stronger, fitter, healthier, and perhaps more intelligent society.

In this chapter, supporting exercise and fitness will be presented with fun challenges called Max 60. This refers to one-minute activities in which students try to get their maximum repetitions while racing against the clock for 60 seconds. Partner Max 60 exercises combine two or more student scores together to see who has the highest total in the class. The goal in these activities is to work as hard as possible with the intention of improving one's fitness level. Additionally, as a second bonus, this will also set the brain for improved academic success. Max 60 challenges will include both individual and partner challenges to increase motivation, teamwork, and excitement. These individual and partner activities are so quick that their implementation could be daily or weekly at the very least. The academic benefits are worth the 60 seconds that are given to improve students' overall health.

Max 60 activities will be well received in your classroom as students will enjoy putting down the pencils and taking a much-needed academic break. These challenges are invigorating to the body and brain. After 60 seconds, students will feel alert, rejuvenated, and ready to conquer their next challenge. Some movements are more difficult than others and result in a greater increase in heart rate or muscular output. However, all activities are vigorous but easily modified to fit various levels.

WHAT ARE SOME BASIC ELEMENTS OF MOVEMENT THAT CAN BE USED EFFECTIVELY IN A CLASSROOM ENVIRONMENT WITH MAX 60?

There are many different ways to move a body. Unfortunately, people of all fitness levels continually tend to repeat the same or similar activities. Take, for instance, an avid runner. Can individuals who choose running as their only source of exercise still improve their fitness levels? Of course they can; however, what might happen if a runner abruptly changes his or her workout and participates in a kickboxing class? Chances are he or she will be sore the next day because his or her body is not used to kickboxing. What does this have to do with movement in the classroom?

It is healthy to move the body in many different ways through various activities and exercises. As you begin to support exercise and fitness, variety will offer novelty. Remember, the brain seeks novelty. There are three distinct categories of movement: (1) locomotor, (2) nonlocomotor, and (3) manipulative skills. As you view nontraditional ways to encourage students to move, ask the question: How and when can I use this during my lessons?

Locomotor movements refer to traveling skills that allow a person to go from one point to another. The most common locomotor movements are walking and jogging. Although walking is very suitable for a classroom environment, there are five suggested movements to consider. These five locomotor skills are as follows:

1. Skip

2. Slide

3. Gallop

4. Hop

5. Leap

Imagine asking your students to skip or gallop to the whiteboard to solve a math problem. This would be an easy request on your part, and many students would love it! If you have ever seen a group of people skipping (any age), you may also have noticed them smiling. It is hard to frown when you are skipping and galloping. These locomotor movements tend to bring pleasure. Choosing a locomotor skill other than walking may make activities more enjoyable and memorable. Be sure to consider your space and the typical speed of the movement.

Nonlocomotor skills are performed in place. Many activities help develop these skills. Here are five examples of nonlocomotor movements that would work effectively in a classroom:

1. Shake

2. Twist

3. Stretch

4. Bend

5. Swing

If you are searching for a simple break in your classroom, put on some music, and teach your students the twist, or allow them to get up and stretch if they have been sitting for longer than 15 to 20 minutes. These nonlocomotor movements are quick and fun to implement. Many of your creative students will enjoy the numerous activities you can generate with nonlocomotor actions.

Manipulative movements include activities that develop gross motor skills. Gross motor skills involve large muscle groups or movement of the whole body. Activities that build manipulative skills are engaging for many students. Kinesthetic learners typically love to use their bodies to learn a skill or perform a physical task. Many different movements can be used to improve gross motor skills. Here are a few examples appropriate for the classroom:

1. Throw/catch

2. Bounce/dribble

3. Volley

4. Balance

5. Push/pull

This book provides many activities to develop locomotor, nonlocomotor, and manipulative skills while performing Max 60 exercises. Max 60 activities provide a large variety of movements that will allow for a total body workout. Other forms of movement that benefit gross motor development can also be designed. For example, allowing students to continually throw and catch a ball while practicing their multiplication facts is a notable case in point. An activity such as this can be very motivating. This can be used advantageously while initiating this purpose of movement.

WHAT ARE THE MAX 60 CHALLENGES I CAN IMPLEMENT IN MY CLASSROOM IN TWO MINUTES OR LESS?

To gain a better understanding of how to engage students in Max 60 exercises, it is beneficial to be familiar with the health-related components of fitness. These components are designed to promote healthy living. The three components addressed in this book are the following:

1. Cardiorespiratory endurance

2. Muscular strength and endurance

3. Flexibility

All three of these health-related components of fitness are used in the Max 60 challenges. Becoming familiar with these components will help you deliver well-rounded workouts as you choose which challenges you will do throughout the week. Even if you have students engage in a physical exercise once a week for one minute, each week should present a different activity that provides a new challenge. For example, if you asked students to complete Max 60 push-ups one week, you might try scissors kicks the following week. Muscular challenges focus on the arms, legs, and core regions of the body. Flexibility activities will be addressed through yoga poses and challenges. Yoga is a beautiful form of exercise that not only improves flexibility but has many other benefits such as increasing muscular strength and endurance, respiration, and cardio and circulatory health, just to name a few. This chapter will contain the following 57 challenges and/or activities:

1. 14 Max 60 Muscular Challenges (seven individual, seven partner)

2. 14 Max 60 Cardiorespiratory Challenges (seven individual, seven partner)

3. 14 Max 60 Yoga Challenges (seven individual, seven partner)

4. 10 Max 60 Sport Challenges (five individual, five partner)

5. 5 Fitness Challenges/Games

MAX 60 MUSCULAR CHALLENGES

Individual

1. Push-ups
   - Have students place their hands on the floor, slightly more than shoulder width apart.
   - They straighten their bodies like a board to balance on their hands and toes.
   - They bend their elbows to lower their bodies to the ground.
   - They go down toward the floor and then push back up.
   - Modification: Place knees on the ground (remember to keep the body straight like a board) or wall push-ups (same rules apply—just push off the wall instead of the floor).

2. Chair Dips
   - Have each student sit on the edge of a chair.
   - Next have them wrap their hands around the chair.
   - Then they lift their bodies off the chair and lower their bodies to the floor directly in front of the chair.
   - They should keep their knees bent and feet flat on the floor (they can straighten their legs to present a greater challenge).
   - When the upper arms become parallel to the floor, students straighten their arms so that they are holding their bodies above the seat of the chair.

○ Do not allow them to touch their buttocks the chair.

○ Modification: Don't bend the arms as far, and rest on the chair between repetitions.

3. Air Squats
   ○ Have students stand with their feet shoulder width apart (or a bit wider).
   ○ They should keep their backs straight and look upward slightly.
   ○ Next they bend knees to lower their buttocks closer to the floor.
   ○ When the top of the legs are parallel to the ground, they stand up.
   ○ They should not bend too low on this exercise.
   ○ Students only bend down until the top leg is parallel with the ground.
   ○ Modification: Do not bend down as far.

4. Lunge
   ○ Have students stand in a wide, staggered stance with hips turned toward the front leg.
   ○ Next they bend the front knee so that it is directly above the foot (they should not allow the knee to pass by the foot).
   ○ Have students keep their back legs fairly straight.
   ○ They should slightly bend the back knee as it moves closer to the ground.
   ○ Just before the knee touches the ground, students slowly head back to the standing stance.
   ○ Remember to have students do the same number of repetitions on each leg.
   ○ Modification: Do not bend down as far.

5. Wall Seat
   ○ Find a wall.
   ○ Have students place their backs against the wall and bend their knees until their upper legs are parallel with the floor.
   ○ They should keep their feet planted flat on the ground.
   ○ Students hold this position for a designated time.
   ○ Modification: Do not bend down as far.

6. Ab Twist
   ○ Students sit their bottoms on the floor with their heels slightly touching the floor.
   ○ They lean backward toward the floor (the further back they lean, the more difficult the challenge).
   ○ Have students interlock their fingers and twist to the right until their hands touch the ground.
   ○ Then they twist to the left the same way while continuing back and forth.
   ○ Modification: Don't lean back or twist as far.

7. Back Crunch
   - Have students straighten their bodies on the floor, facing down.
   - They should place their arms directly out in front.
   - At the same time, they lift the right arm and the left leg off the ground and into the air as high as they can.
   - Remember to have them keep arms and legs straight.
   - Then they lift the left arm with the right leg and continue.
   - Modification: Perform the activity standing flat against a wall, or don't lift arms and legs as high.

Partner

8. Shoulder Taps
   - Have partners in a push-up-ready position (bodies straight like a board).
   - They should tap or fist bump one another with their right hands in the center space between them.
   - Then, they tap or fist bump with the left hand and continue.
   - Modification: Place knees on the ground while keeping the body straight.

9. Chair Dip Seesaw
   - Have partners sit on the edge of a chair, facing one another.
   - Each person wraps his or her hands around the chair.
   - Then they lift their bodies off the chair: one lowers his or her body to the floor directly in front of the chair, while the other partner stays up.
   - They should keep knees bent and feet flat on the floor (they can straighten legs to present a greater challenge).
   - When the upper arms become parallel to the floor, they straighten their arms so that they are holding their bodies above the seat of the chair.
   - They should not allow their buttocks to touch the chair.
   - When one partner comes up, the other one goes down, like a seesaw.
   - Modification: Don't bend the arms as far, and rest on the chair when it's the partner's turn.

10. Partner Squats
    - Have students stand with their feet shoulder width apart (or a bit wider), while facing one another.
    - They connect hands in the center.
    - They should keep backs straight and look upward slightly.
    - At the same time, partners bend their knees to lower buttocks closer to the floor.

- When the top of their legs are parallel to the ground, both partners stand back up.
- Students should not bend too low on this exercise.
- They should bend down only until the top leg is parallel with the ground.
- Modification: Do not bend down as far, and partners can slow their speed.

11. Partner Lunges
    - Have partners stand side by side in a wide, staggered stance with hips turned toward the front leg.
    - Partners will put their hands on one another's inner shoulders (this will help for balancing).
    - Students bend their front knees at the same time so that they are directly above the front foot (they should not allow the knees to pass by the front foot).
    - Have students keep their back legs fairly straight.
    - Next, they begin to slightly bend their back knees as they move closer to the ground.
    - Just before their knees touch the ground, the partners slowly head back to the standing stance.
    - Remember to have students do the same number of repetitions on each leg.
    - Modification: Partners should not bend down as far or slow their speed.

12. Squat Hold
    - Partners stand facing one another.
    - They connect hands in the center.
    - At the same time, they bend their knees until their upper legs are parallel with the floor.
    - Student should keep feet planted flat on the ground.
    - Both partners hold this position for a designated time, using one another for balance and support.
    - Modification: Do not bend down as far.

13. Back-to-Back Pass
    - Have partners stand back to back.
    - One partner will twist left to pass a ball or object to his or her partner.
    - The other partner twists right to receive it then left to pass it.
    - Students switch directions on the teacher's command.
    - Modification: Decrease speed when passing the object, or sit on the floor back to back.

14. Partner Row
    - Have students sit on the floor while facing a partner.
    - Partners link hands and touch toes in the center space between them.

- One partner leans back, while at the same time the other partner is leaning forward.
- Partners then switch roles.
- Remember to have students keep their hands connected and toes touching.
- Modification: Do not lean back as far, and decrease speed.

MAX 60 CARDIORESPIRATORY CHALLENGES

Individual

1. Scissors Kicks
   - Have students begin by placing their arms on their hips and staggering their feet one in front of the other.
   - Students jump and switch the positions of the feet; then they continue jumping and switching feet.
   - Modification: Switch feet without jumping.

2. Mountain Climbers
   - Have students place their hands on the floor directly underneath their shoulders.
   - Then they stagger feet so that one foot is placed on the floor beneath the chest with a bent knee, and the other leg is straightened (students should get on their toes).
   - They jump and switch the positions of their feet.
   - Next they continue to switch feet.
   - Modification: Do not jump when switching feet. Perform air climber (standing up, with the right arm and left knee in the air, then the left arm with right knee—continue).

3. Jump Twists
   - Have students stand with their hips facing forward.
   - Next they jump and twist their hips to the right.
   - Then they jump and go back to the forward position.
   - And next they jump and twist their hips to the left.
   - They follow the pattern forward, right, forward, and left.
   - Modification: Twist by using quick steps instead of jumping.

4. Heel Kicks
   - Have students jog in place, bringing the heels of their feet back to their buttocks with each step.
   - Modification: Slow the speed to a walking pace.

5. Hop Scotch
   - Have students stand on two feet, hop, and then stand on just the right foot.
   - Then they hop on two feet and stand on the left foot.

○ Have them continue the pattern of hop (two feet), right foot, hop, then left foot.
○ Modification: Lift to the toes instead of hopping.

6. High Knee Hold
   ○ Have students stand on two feet to start.
   ○ Next they lean to the right and put weight on the right leg.
   ○ At the same time, they lift the left leg high while grabbing the left ankle, hold for a second, and then release.
   ○ Then have them lean to the left side and lift the right leg high, grab the right ankle, hold, and release.
   ○ Modification: Lift the leg to a comfortable height and hold.

7. Toe Kicks
   ○ Have students stand on two feet, kick the left leg up, and touch the toe with the right fingers (while trying to keep their legs straight).
   ○ Then they get back on two feet, then kick the right leg up, and touch the toes with the left fingers.
   ○ Have them continue with the pattern.
   ○ Modification: Use a slower speed and bend the knee while lifting it, or touch the thigh instead of the toes.

Partner

1. Jumping Jack Scarf Clap
   ○ Give partners a scarf, and have them face one another.
   ○ Partner 1 throws the scarf into the air.
   ○ Once in the air, partner 2 does one jumping jack and catches it.
   ○ Then they switch roles.
   ○ Every time a partner makes a successful catch, they add another jumping jack the next time it is their turn.
   ○ Modification: Step instead of jumping, and use higher tosses to give your partner more time.

2. Seesaw Squat Jump
   ○ Have one partner bend down and touch hands to the floor while keeping the back straight, head up, and feet shoulder width apart.
   ○ The other partner stays standing.
   ○ Next, the partner who bent down jumps high into the air (raising his or her hands to the ceiling).
   ○ Then the partner who was standing bends down and does the same thing, while the other person remains standing (seesaw); they continue with the up-and-down pattern.
   ○ Modification: Go onto the toes instead of jumping, and decrease speed.

3. Alternate Line Jumps
   - Have partners find a line on the floor (it can be imaginary).
   - One partner starts on one side of the line, while the other partner is on the other side.
   - While keeping their feet together and continuing to face one another, each partner jumps to the other side of the line.
   - They continue jumping side to side across the line at the same speed.
   - Modification: Step across the line as opposed to jumping, and decrease speed.

4. High Knee Alternate
   - Have partners face one another approximately shoulder width apart.
   - At the same time, the partners lift the right knee (until the thigh is parallel to the ground) and tap it with the right hand.
   - Then they lift the left knee and tap it.
   - Partners must move together in unison.
   - Modification: Do not lift leg as high, and decrease speed.

5. In/Out Jumps
   - Partners face one another.
   - One partner has his or her feet apart, while the other keeps his or her feet together to start.
   - At the same time, both students jump and switch the positions of their feet (out comes in, and in goes out).
   - Students must move together at the same speed in unison.
   - Modification: Step out instead of jumping, and decrease speed.

6. Alternating Squat Punches
   - Partners stand in a squatted position while facing one another a little more than shoulder width apart.
   - Both students air punch toward one another at the same time with the right arm and then with the left.
   - Partners must move together in unison.
   - Modification: Do not squat as deeply, and decrease speed.

7. Alternating Squat Kicks
   - Partners stand facing one another approximately three to four feet apart.
   - Both students squat, then stand, and air kick at the same time with the right leg, then squat, stand, and air kick with the left.
   - Have students follow the pattern of squat, stand, right kick, squat, stand, and left kick.
   - Partners must move together in unison.
   - Modification: Do not squat as deeply, and decrease height of kick and speed.

MAX 60 YOGA CHALLENGES

Individual

1. Mountain Pose
   - Have students stand straight with feet together or hip width apart.
   - Students tighten their legs and slightly tuck the tailbone under.
   - They should not lock knees.
   - Have students stand tall with a straight spine, arms hanging down and palms facing upward.
   - Ask them to engage the body and relax the mind.
   - Modification: Slightly widen the legs.

2. Warrior 2
   - Have students stand with feet three to four feet apart.
   - Students raise the arms parallel to the floor and reach them out to the sides with palms facing down.
   - Have students turn the right foot slightly to the right and the left foot out to the left 90 degrees.
   - They should align the heels.
   - Next, they align the left kneecap with the center of the left ankle.
   - Then they bend the knee over the left ankle while straightening the right leg and pressing the heel to the ground.
   - Have them stretch the shoulder blades wide and keep the shoulders directly over the pelvis.
   - Next they should turn the head to the left and look out over the fingers.
   - Then they do the same thing on the other side.
   - Modification: Soften the bend in the knees.

3. Triangle Pose
   - Have students stand with legs approximately three feet apart.
   - Next they turn the right toes to the right wall and the left toes slightly inward.
   - Then they press the left hips out to the left while sliding both arms parallel to the floor.
   - Have students rotate the arms by raising the left arm up and resting the right hand against that right leg, with the palms facing downward.
   - They should keep the body strong while reaching the fingertips away from one another and placing the arms in a straight line (with shoulders stacked).
   - Then they press the left hip forward and the right hip back.
   - Make sure they do the same thing on the other side.
   - Modification: Do not reach the hand as low to the floor.

4. Crescent Moon
   o Have students begin in Mountain Pose.
   o They interlace their fingers and raise their arms over their heads.
   o Have them stand tall while relaxing the shoulders.
   o Next, they press the right hip out to the side while arching over to the left.
   o They should engage the body while reaching up through the body.
   o Then have them do the same thing on the other side.
   o Modification: Soften the arch to a more comfortable level.

5. High Lunge
   o Have students place their hands on the floor while stepping the right foot forward between the hands, aligning the knee over the heel.
   o Then they raise the torso upright and sweep the arms overhead (with palms facing one another).
   o Next they lengthen the tailbone and reach back through the left heel.
   o They should look up toward their thumbs.
   o Then have them do the same thing on the other side.
   o Modification: Do not go as deep into the bend.

6. Standing Backbend
   o Have students stand with feet hip distance apart.
   o They should extend the arms up overhead and bring the palms together.
   o Have them keep weight balanced on both feet and relax the shoulders down.
   o They should engage the thighs, relax the buttocks, and push the hips forward.
   o Next, they lift and broaden the sternum while bending back from the torso.
   o Then they extend the arms along the ears and, if it doesn't hurt the neck, gaze forward or upward.
   o Modification: Do not go as deeply into the bend.

7. Standing Forward Bend
   o Have students stand with feet together.
   o They should slightly bend the knees and fold the torso over the legs, moving from the hips (not the back).
   o Next they place the hands next to the feet on the ground in front of the body.
   o Then they lengthen the spine and gaze forward.
   o Have them straighten their legs without locking them.
   o Then they extend downward without rounding the back.
   o And then they extend the head and neck toward the ground.
   o Modification: Reach as low as the body allows.

Partner

1. V Pose
   - ○ Partners stand facing one another with feet fairly close together.
   - ○ Students hold hands, and slowly start to lean backward.
   - ○ Hold pose in the letter V.
   - ○ Modification: Increase the distance between the feet.

2. Y Pose
   - ○ Partners stand facing one another approximately a foot apart.
   - ○ Student will keep their legs straight, lifting the torso from the hips, and gently bend backward.
   - ○ Form the letter Y, and hold.
   - ○ Modification: Gently bend the torso to a comfortable level.

3. Parallel Seat
   - ○ Partners stand facing one another with hands held and arms extended.
   - ○ Then sit in a squatted position until both students' thighs are parallel to the ground.
   - ○ Then they balance and hold.
   - ○ Modification: Do not squat as deeply.

4. Twin Trees
   - ○ Partners stand next to one another.
   - ○ They bring one side of the hips together.
   - ○ Then they lift opposite legs away from one another other and guide them into the inner thigh.
   - ○ Next they lift the inner arms overhead and touch palms.
   - ○ Then the partners lift the outer arms up to the sides for balance.
   - ○ Have them do the same thing on the other side.
   - ○ Modification: Lift the leg only to the ankle or calf muscle.

5. Supported Warrior
   - ○ Partners stand in the warrior pose already described.
   - ○ Instead of lifting both arms, they place their inner arms on one another's shoulders.
   - ○ Then they lift the outer arms into the air.
   - ○ Have them do the same thing on the other side.
   - ○ Modification: Bend only to a level of comfort.

6. Partner Dance
   - ○ Partners stand facing one another and bring left palms touching together overhead.
   - ○ They lift the right leg behind them and hold onto the foot.
   - ○ They balance one another and hold.
   - ○ Have them lift the leg as high as possible.
   - ○ Modification: Lift the leg to a comfortable level.

7. Partner Mountain
   ○ Partners stand back to back with feet together or hip width apart.
   ○ They tighten their legs and slightly tuck their tailbones under.
   ○ They should not lock their knees.
   ○ Have students stand tall with a straight spine, arms hanging down, and palms facing upward.
   ○ Partners engage the body and relax the mind.
   ○ Ask the partners to use their posture to strengthen each other.
   ○ Modification: Slightly widen the legs.

MAX 60 SPORT CHALLENGES

Individual and Partner

(The physical activity is the same movement, but the individual challenge consists of one score, and the partner challenge is a combination of two or more scores.)

1. Basketball Shooting
   ○ Have students pretend to receive an imaginary pass as they jump and shoot the basketball into the basket.
   ○ Partners can move at different speeds.
   ○ Modification: Lift onto the toes instead of jumping, and decrease speed.

2. Soccer Toe Taps
   ○ Have students pretend to tap their right foot, then their left foot, onto an imagery soccer ball between their feet.
   ○ Partners can move at their own speed.
   ○ Modification: Decrease the speed of the taps.

3. Volleyball Blocks
   ○ Have students raise their arms overhead and jump as though they are blocking a spike in a volleyball game.
   ○ Partners can move at their own speed.
   ○ Modification: Lift onto the toes instead of jumping, and decrease speed.

4. Football Tire Drill
   ○ Have students lift the right leg, like they are running through tires, then the left.
   ○ Partners can move at their own speed.
   ○ Modification: Decrease the speed to a walk.

5. Speed Skaters
   ○ Have students bend their knees and jump while swinging the right leg backward behind the left leg.

o Then, they jump again and place the left leg behind the right (looking like a speed skater).
o Partners can move at their own speed.
o Modification: Decrease speed, and eliminate the jump.

FITNESS CHALLENGES/GAMES

1. Fitness Scavenger Hunt (see Figure 8.1)
   o Any exercises can be used to replace the ones listed on the sample sheet provided.
   o Modifications have already been given.

2. Sports Relay
   o Place students in groups of four.
   o Have two team members on one side of the room and the other two on the other side of the room.
   o This is a drill where a skill is performed and the person who performed it goes across the room and gets in the line on the other side of the room.
   o Many skills can be used, such as tossing a football, passing a soccer ball, rolling a softball grounder, or performing a locomotor movement.
   o For example, player 1 and 2 are on one side of the room, and player 3 and 4 are on the other side. Player 1 tosses a ball to player 3 and then speed walks across the room to get behind player 4. Next, player 3 tosses the ball to player 2 and speed walks to get behind her.
   o Modification: Slower speeds, closer distances, and softer or larger equipment can be used.

3. Tunnel Hockey
   o Split the class into two teams, and have them stand in two straight lines six to ten feet apart, facing one another.
   o Have students spread their feet to make tunnels with their legs (with teammates' feet touching one another).
   o Students will pretend their hands are hockey sticks.
   o Students must stay standing and bend their knees to tap the balls.
   o Use numerous balls in the game. Team 1 will try and tap the balls under team 2's tunnels and vice versa.
   o Students can leave the line they formed at any time to retrieve balls that get behind them (although their line will then have a weak link).
   o When the teacher says, "Freeze," the team with the most balls on their side loses the round.
   o Play multiple rounds.
   o Modification: Use a softer bend in the knees throughout the game, and give rest breaks between rounds.

Figure 8.1

FITNESS SCAVENGER HUNT

Sample Sheet

Please find a peer who is able and willing to perform the given task/challenge for you. He or she must physically attempt and complete the activity before signing off on your sheet. After someone completes the exercise, he or she can sign only one paper. The first person with a completed sheet is the winner.

1. 10 Jumping Jacks_____

2. 10 Push-ups_____

3. 20 Scissor Kicks_____

4. 2 Jump Tucks_____

5. 10 Windmills_____

6. 10 Mountain Climbers_____

7. 10 Back Crunches (against a wall)_____

8. 10 Cross-Laterals_____

9. 20 Air Punches_____

10. 5 Chair Push-ups_____

11. 6 Lunges (3 on each leg)_____

12. 8 Quad Burners (Squats)_____

13. 2 360-degree Spins (one in each direction)_____

14. 5 Star Jumps_____

15. 10 Butt Kicks_____

16. 10 Hops (on the right foot), 10 Hops (on the left)_____

17. 3 Burpees_____

18. Hold a 10-second Plank_____

19. Stand in a One-Legged Yoga Pose for 10 Seconds_____

20. 10 Crunches (or other ab exercise)_____

4. Bean Bag Challenge
   o Give each student a bean bag.
   o Have the students perform multiple challenges with the bean bags.
   o Some examples are to pass the beanbag around different body parts (head, waist, legs, or ankles, or combine all body parts), figure eights, toss-spin-catch, balance on hand flips, and so on.
   o Get students into pairs, and do partner challenges, such as two-handed catches, one-handed catches, or various types of throws, and add multiple bean bag throw/catch challenges.
   o Modification: Allow students to choose their own speed, and use closer distances with partners.

5. Fitness Freeze Tag
   o Have one to four students be the taggers, and give them something to tag with, such as a ball or shortened noodle.
   o Set a designated boundary area.
   o Remind students they can't move faster than a walk.
   o Students will move around the area while trying to avoid the taggers.
   o If a student is tagged, he or she is frozen.
   o Everyone can unfreeze themselves by performing a given exercise 10 times.
   o Change taggers every minute or so.
   o Modification: Perform fewer exercises or easier ones.

Max 60 challenges are fun and easy to implement. By having students perform these weekly or daily, the Kinesthetic Educator can truly play a role in improving the physical health and fitness of his or her students. These activities are sure to reenergize the brain while also giving it a break from academic content. The increase in heart rate will result in better blood flow to the brain and fresh oxygen that will allow for a clearer learning state. When used appropriately, these Max 60 challenges can allow for total body exercises throughout a week's time in your classroom. Ultimately, fitness levels will improve in our younger generations, and academic scores will rise in unison. This harmonic state seems to be one we all should be able to agree on.

HOW CAN EXERCISE AND FITNESS BE SUPPORTED IN MY CLASSROOM IF I AM NOT CURRENTLY ACTIVE IN MY OWN LIFE?

As previously mentioned the health and well-being of our society has taken a nose dive for our younger generation; however, adults are not an exception. Most Americans lead inactive lives and have an unhealthy diet that is damaging and detrimental. The choice to be physically fit is yours alone. Maintaining a high level of fitness takes a great deal of time and effort. Exercise is hard work and is often perceived as boring. These feelings are typical for adults, adolescents, and children alike. There are many reasons for making exercise and fitness a part of your everyday routine; the most important is your health and well-being. Human nature desires a healthy mind, body, and soul. However, teachers have a serious time commitment to their profession. For many, the result is no time available for exercising. Or is there?

Implementing exercise and fitness in your classroom is a perfect opportunity to make life changes for both you and your students. You can incorporate exercise into your lessons and join your students to receive the benefits as well. This would be an achievable place to begin making small changes to your own life. This fitness commitment can be made by simply setting a goal to involve your students, along with yourself, in physical activities for one or two minutes every school day. Everyone has a minute to give to exercise! This minute can be built into your classroom schedule. You might then consider extending this exercise regimen to your personal life. There are many fitness challenges provided earlier in this chapter, each taking two minutes or less. Engaging in these is a great opportunity to make changes for both yourself and your students.

If you're saying to yourself, "But I hate exercise," remember this feeling is common and acceptable. Many of your students are sharing these exact feelings. Think about all the responsibilities you endure. Do you enjoy all of them? Of course not! By supporting exercise and fitness in your classroom, you are providing yourself with time to exercise while reenergizing your students. Therefore, lack of time can no longer be your excuse or your students.' Now all you need is the motivation! Allow your students to motivate you, as you in turn motivate them. Explain to your students that the goal is to develop healthy habits about exercise and fitness. In turn, you become an important role model, as do they.

Supporting exercise and fitness in your classroom does have a distinct purpose for setting the learner's brain for peak performance. This opportunity is not just opening the door for you to incorporate exercise into your life and your students; it is also providing a brain break and boost to enhance academic success. Also, as explained in Chapter 1, physically fit children are performing better academically. The increased oxygen and blood to the brain wake up both the body and brain to boost the learning process, also perhaps improving your teaching. The important message about fitness will be clearly heard when all teachers in a school building support exercise and fitness in the classroom as well as in the gymnasium. Imagine how physically exhausted your students will be at the end of the day. The educators have the ability to take inactive life habits and support exercise and fitness to improve their own overall health and well-being as well as that of their students.

If you have physical or personal reasons why you are not exercising (or students with these same concerns), you can still support fitness in your classroom. Hanging a poster in your room that describes and shows the exercise challenges is an initial place to begin. It is realistic to assume that you have at least one or more students in your classroom who are familiar with the exercises and would be willing to demonstrate them for the class. Also, one amazing aspect of fitness is the numerous modifications that can be made to just about every exercise, therefore allowing everyone to participate at his or her own level.

Students might truly enjoy being asked to come to the front of the room, choose an exercise from the poster, and lead their classmates through the challenge for one minute. Many students will be motivated by this opportunity simply to get out of their seats. Students who are not motivated would be more comfortable following the leader. Either way, students are moving, exercising, and building healthy habits.

CHAPTER SUMMARY

- In this chapter, supporting exercise and fitness were presented with fun challenges called Max 60. This refers to one-minute activities where students try to get their maximum repetitions while racing against the clock for 60 seconds. Partner Max 60 exercises combine two or more students' scores together to see who has the highest total in the class.
- There are three distinct categories of movement: (1) locomotor, (2) nonlocomotor, and (3) manipulative skills.
- Max 60 activities provide a large variety of movements that will allow for a total body workout.
- The health-related components of fitness are: cardiorespiratory endurance, muscular strength and endurance, and flexibility. Max 60 challenges can be used to improve each component.
- This chapter contains 57 challenges and/or activities: 14 Max 60 Muscular Challenges (seven individual, seven partner), 14 Max 60 Cardiorespiratory Challenges (seven individual, seven partner), 14 Max 60 Yoga Challenges (seven individual, seven partner), 10 Max 60 Sport Challenges (five individual, five partner), and five Fitness Challenges/Games.
- Muscular challenges focus on the arms, legs, and core regions of the body. Flexibility activities are addressed through yoga poses and challenges.
- Max 60 challenges are fun and easy to implement. By having students perform these weekly or daily, the Kinesthetic Educator can truly play a role in improving the physical health and fitness of his or her students.

- Implementing exercise and fitness in your classroom is a perfect opportunity to make life changes for both you and your students. You can incorporate exercise into your lessons and join your students to receive the benefits as well.
- Supporting exercise and fitness in your classroom does have a distinct purpose for setting the learner's brain for peak performance.

TIPS FOR THE STAFF DEVELOPER

Don't be intimidated to try Max 60 exercises with your participants. Ask them to dress comfortably and participate as they want and can. You might also want to do some research on target heart rates to share with your audience. Much of the literature on aerobic activity, physical fitness, and academic achievement focuses on this. Target heart rate information is more for the physical educator than classroom teacher, but it is always good information for teachers on both a personal and professional level to be an advocate for more daily, quality, and fitness-oriented physical education in schools.

PART 4

———

Go

Uniting Movement and Academics

9

Reviewing Content

⇨ What are the benefits of reviewing content through movement?

⇨ How much time should be spent reviewing content through movement?

⇨ What are 15 movement activities that can be used to review academic content?

WHAT ARE THE BENEFITS OF REVIEWING CONTENT THROUGH MOVEMENT?

Rehearsal, the repetitive act of processing information, is critical for transferring content from working memory to long-term storage (Sousa, 2017). Using movement to review content is a form of elaborative rehearsal, which often engages higher-order thinking skills and/or greater sensory input. Other benefits of reviewing content using movement include the following:

- Getting the benefit of a brain break (greater blood flow, etc.) without having to take one
- Engagement by all in the review process
- An emotionally safe way to be involved with review
- With the right activity, can be used as an immediate assessment tool
- The possibility of anchoring a correct answer with a movement activity

HOW MUCH TIME SHOULD BE SPENT REVIEWING CONTENT THROUGH MOVEMENT?

Taking time to review content is an essential aspect of the teaching and learning process. Student needs differ concerning how often they require exposure to a particular concept before it is learned and stored. Many students rely on teachers to review information for recall to become more efficient. This process allows the brain to create sense or meaning that aids in retrieval.

Reviewing content in some form should happen on a consistent basis. A common question is how often to use movement during review. The answer depends on availability of time and type of movement activity being considered. Some activities are quickly implemented, whereas others require more time, student involvement, and teacher-directed instruction.

WHAT ARE 15 MOVEMENT ACTIVITIES THAT CAN BE USED TO REVIEW ACADEMIC CONTENT?

1. Brain Snatch
   Students will be split into five equal teams of three to six on a team.
   - You may have fewer teams if you have a smaller class.
   - Each team stands in a separate corner of the room. One team is in the middle of the room.
   - Colored cards containing answers for the review guides are spread all around the center of the room.
   - Each team sends one person to the center of the room to snatch a designated color card, for example, blue. The team on the inside is holding tagging noodles (pool noodles).
   - If the team member who goes into the center to get a blue card gets tagged by a person with a noodle, he or she goes back to his or her corner and sends another person back in to try to get a card.
   - If someone gets a card back home without getting tagged, he or she uses the answer on the card to fill in an answer on the review sheet.
   - Make sure one member of a team goes into the game at a time and everyone has an equal turn.
   - A team must be the first one to complete their study guide and have all answers correct before they win the game.
   - Rotate corners, so each team will now have a new study guide, and they will go after a different set of colored cards to find their answers.
   - The teacher must spread the cards out in the center between each game.
   - A new tagging team will have the noodles for each game.
   - Due to space, if the game is too easy for the taggers, have them partner up and stay linked when they tag people coming in for the cards. You can even link people in threes if need be.

○ Be sure to review the walking rule before each game, and make sure participants understand proper use of the noodles. No one is trying to hit a home run!

2. Challenge Flash Review
   ○ Split the class into two to four groups depending on the class size (about three to eight in a group).
   ○ Give a review question to the entire class.
   ○ Each team will huddle up and come up with a team answer.
   ○ Each team will have a recorder who will write the answer on a piece of paper. Each team should have a new recorder for each challenge.
   ○ After the answer is written, the recorder will say, "Go." Each team will race to complete a given challenge that is designated prior to reading the review question. For example, the challenge may be 10 jumping jacks. The teacher states the challenge and then reads the review questions.
   ○ Teams huddle and give their answer to their recorder. He or she writes the answer down on the paper and says, "Go." The team will stand, complete the challenge together (e.g., 10 jumping jacks), then sit.
   ○ The first team sitting will receive two points for a correct answer. Other teams will receive one point for the correct answer.
   ○ Continue the game with different review questions and various challenges. Challenge suggestions are listed as follows.

   Challenges
   a. 10 jumping jacks
   b. Pass a penny around a circle two times
   c. Pass a ball around a circle three times
   d. Pass a ball around a circle one time with an elbow-to-elbow pass (ball pinched between the elbows)
   e. Tunnel roll (with the group in circle, make a tunnel with their feet apart and roll a ball on the ground through the tunnel)
   f. Over-under relay in a circle two times
   g. 20 scissors kicks
   h. Washing machine in a circle two times (twist left, twist right)
   i. 26 punches (alternate right and left)
   j. Star pass (ball gets passed in a star-like pattern where players can't throw the ball to the players on their immediate right or left)

3. Gallery Walk With Review Questions
   ○ Have students do a gallery walk, in a clockwise or counterclockwise motion, with review questions posted (on cards, poster paper, etc.) around the room.
   ○ Make sure there is one question per student in the class.
   ○ The objective is for the students to answer as many questions as possible in a given amount of time.
   ○ Review question answers with the whole class.

4. Body Webbing
   - Give each student some note cards, and assign them to read a certain preassigned story.
   - Make sure you have an even split of students reading each of the different stories (16 participants, four stories = four participants reading one story).
   - Working individually, students will read their stories and write what they think the main ideas are on note cards, and tape them to their stomachs (which is the center or main part of the body).
   - They will then continue to write key details on the note cards and tape them to their limbs (also important parts of the body but not the main section of the body like the stomach is).
   - Groups detailing the same stories will then get together to compare answers.
   - Each group will share their answers with the entire class while discussing any differences within their groups.
   - This activity can also be used to springboard into teaching summarizing. It has individual thought processing, group work, and class collaboration wrapped into one.

5. Square Dance Discussion Circle
   - Ask students to write a list of five things that are important to them.
   - Under each idea, students will list supporting reasons why it is important to them.
   - Then create an inside/outside circle (or line if space is tight).
   - Participants on the inside circle will match up with a participant from the outside circle.
   - Introduce some basic square dance moves for fun, and allow the students to practice them (see Square Dance Calls, p. 139).
   - Then instruct the group on the inside of the circle to start a conversation by telling their partners about something that is important to them and why.
   - It is the responsibility of those on the outside to continue the conversation while adding their thoughts and opinions.
   - Discuss the importance of good discussion techniques (eye contact, respectful listening, open-minded listening, etc.).
   - Allow for a two- to three-minute discussion. Then have students practice some more square dance moves again.
   - After a few minutes, allow participants to match up with a new partner, while the inner person will start the conversation again. (The inner circle should always be changing as they do-si-do and swing their partners.) Continue for a few rounds of discussion, with square dance practice in between rounds.

Square Dance Calls
a. Circle (left/right)—inner and outer groups move in opposite directions.
b. Swing your partner—with elbows linked, spin one and a half turns, so students switch which circle they are in.
c. Do-si-do—back-to-back partners circle one another while switching which circle they are in.
d. Bow to your partner/corner—this is self-explanatory.
e. Promenade—circles move in the same direction.

○ The discussion circle has been in existence for a very long time. However, few teachers use it in their classrooms. It is easy to implement, little space is needed, noise is minimal, and students have the opportunity to engage with their classmates respectively. Why not take advantage of this simple, long-forgotten technique that has great value? Plus adding the square dance move is a great way to have some fun and build class cohesion.

6. The AP Line Jump
   ○ Explain active and passive voice.
   ○ Split class into two to four even teams depending on the size.
   ○ Use masking tape to make two to four lines in the classroom.
   ○ Each team stands on their line.
   ○ The teacher reads a sentence.
   ○ Students will jump to the left of the line for active and to the right of the line for passive while saying the verb at the same time.
   ○ Teams can decide to jump together as a joint decision, which means they would get all of the points if they are correct or none if they are incorrect.
   ○ They can also choose to jump as individuals, which may result in some team members on both sides of the tape (a point is given for each team member on the correct side of the line).
   ○ Play the game with five sentences while keeping a running total of points.
   ○ Then have students close their eyes and play the game as individuals while keeping their own score.

7. Content Tag
   ○ Clear a large area in your room.
   ○ Before the tag game begins, place some safety spots in the game boundaries (Hula Hoops or large poster paper will work fine).
   ○ Place several index cards of content review questions.
   ○ While on a safety spot, players are safe from being tagged.
   ○ Also while on a safety spot, students must answer one review question.

- Choose a few players to be "it," allowing them to carry a ball they can use to tag other players.
- If players are not on a safety spot, they will move around the room while trying not to be tagged, they take the ball, and they are now considered to be it.
- If players want to be on a safety spot, they simply step on it and say "C-ya" to the other player on the spot.
- The other player has to get off the spot immediately.
- Note: If large safety spots are used, two players may stand on a spot at one time. In this instance, a player who wants to get onto a safety spot can simply tap the shoulder of just one of the players on a safety spot while saying "C-ya!" (Only the player tapped on the shoulder must get off the safety spot.)

8. Human Transformations
   - Split the class into groups of four to six students.
   - Have them spread out in the classroom.
   - Have each team "construct" a "sculpture" using their bodies.
   - The teacher will give a command—reflect (flip), rotate (spin), or translate (slide)—and each team will perform the operation on their human sculpture.
   - After a few rounds, have student teams construct new "sculptures" and repeat.
   - This activity can serve as a quick formative assessment or as a fun student energizer. Make sure you are using the correct terminology (reflect, rotate, and translate).

9. Five Signs Review
   - Place five signs around the room with the different words representing a topic such as "biomes" (e.g., aquatic, forest, tundra, dessert, and forest).
   - Scatter note cards around the room containing definitions and descriptions of each biome (or other content that you have chosen—include pictures if you would like).
   - Have students mill around the room by themselves or with a partner.
   - They pick up one card at a time to try and match it to the biome by sticking it on the wall at the correct place.
   - Any group can move another group's card if they don't agree.
   - Reflect and review correct answers.
   - You can add a review game here where you read the cards and students go to the correct biome.

10. Water Cycle Tag
    - Scatter balls throughout a large area to represent the atmosphere.
    - Lay out the pool noodles as if you are looking at a cross section of land, make a "hill," "flat land," and another "hill." Finally at the end use noodles to create a "lake."

- The balls will represent the particulate matter in the air. Each section of land will be represented by a physical activity to move through the section.
- Begin with all of the students on "land." Explain that there is always moisture in the air, but they are representing you as the instructor pouring water at the top of a hill.
- When you say, "Go," that represents the sun in the sky, and the water (students) begin to flow.
- To move down the first hill, each student must high step until they reach the next section.
- In the flat section of pool noodles, each student must do lunges to move across to the next section.
- In the final section each student must hop.
- While the students are moving, the instructor will act as their energy directing them to evaporate.
- Randomly, the instructor will tap a student or tell a student that he or she has evaporated into the atmosphere. If a student isn't evaporated by the time he or she reaches the end, he or she collects in the lake.
- The instructor may also tell students in the lake that they have evaporated.
- While in the lake students must perform any physical activity of their choice (jumping jacks, cross crawls, etc.).
- The students who evaporated will go out and grab a ball (attach to particulate).
- Because he or she is not dense enough to precipitate back to Earth, the person with the ball becomes "it" and has to take three other people. Each person tagged will join arms, and they act as one entity.
- Once there are four total people linked, they will precipitate back straight to Earth in the portion of pool noodle "below" them.
- They do not have to directly precipitate at the beginning.
- The person with the ball will place it where he or she lands. The teacher can throw the balls back into the atmosphere by shouting an event that will cause particulate matter to become airborne: a sand storm, sneeze, breeze, dusting, and so on.
- Throughout the cycle the instructor will blow a whistle and shout "night" or "day." During the day the students will move at a normal pace. During the night the students will move at a slower pace.
- The game is over when the teacher chooses it to be.

11. Vocabulary Review
    - Choose a word such as "obstinate."
    - Define it in two or three words such as "hardheaded" and "unyielding."
    - Create a movement for each word of the definition. For "hardheaded" you might hit for fist against your head several times.

For "unyielding" you might use both hands to push away from your body.

o Perform it for your students by saying the words of the definition while doing the movement and repeating the vocabulary word one final time.

o Have students perform with you.

o Finally have your students choose the word (from current content or a predetermined list), create the definition and movements, and teach the rest of the class.

12. The Chaining Game

o Students stand in a circle.

o All students will be given an index card with an answer to a review question at the top of the card (e.g., "9") matched to a particular review question that has been asked by someone else in the group (e.g., "Who has 3 x 3?"—written at the bottom of his or her card). This activity is a closed system where the number of answers and questions is the same.

o The correct answer and its appropriate question will never be on the same card.

o Here is an example of what might be written on one student's card:

"I have the number 9."

"Who has 3 x 4?"

The person who recognizes that the heading at the top of his or her card is the answer to that question would reply, "I have the number 12."

"Who has 4 x 4?" The reply is: "I have 16."

"Who has . . . ?" and on it goes.

o Shuffle the cards, and hand them out again. Play the game several times until all people have a good understanding of the content under review.

13. Block Partners

o Distribute the block partnering template to students (you can vary in number of blocks to your liking).

o Explain that their job is to move around the room and pick a different partner for each of the block's numbered segments. Encourage students to choose partners from outside their own area or table.

- For instance, if Sally asks John to be her number 1 block partner, their names go in each other's number 1 block. That way, when you instruct the students to find their number 1 block partner, each student knows exactly who to find.
- There can be no repeat partners!
- Sally and John then move on to find number 2 block partners, and so on, until all blocks are filled.
- Mathematically it might not work out that students have all blocks completed with a partner's name. If, for instance, you instruct students to find their number 7 block partner and a student does not have a partner for that block, he or she can join with another pair to create a trio for the review.
- Once students are standing and partnered, give them the topic or question for review and discussion.
- This can also be a way to partner students for brain break activities.

14. Relay Review
   - Separate the class so that three or four people are on each team.
   - Have teams line up in the back of the room.
   - When the teacher says, "Go," one person will speed walk to the front of the room to answer a question on the board asked by the teacher.
   - He or she will speed walk back and tag the next person.
   - That person will go to the front of the room to add a fact of some sort to the answer given by the first person.
   - Continue until everyone goes once.
   - Check to see if all groups agree and share the correct or similar answers
   - Award a point to each team for each correct answer.
   - Play three more rounds, each with new questions or content.

15. Word or Number Scramble Review
   - Separate the class into two to five teams depending on the size of the class.
   - Give each team a packet that contains small strips of paper with academic content that is not in a specific order.
   - Teams will race to put their content in the appropriate order.
   - At the end of the race, compare each group's answers.
   - Continue with another challenge/problem for the team to unscramble.

SAMPLE BLOCK PARTNERING ORGANIZER

1	2	3	4
5	6	7	8
9	10	11	12

CHAPTER SUMMARY

- Rehearsal is critical for transferring content from working memory to long-term storage (Sousa, 2017). Using movement to review content is a form of elaborative rehearsal, which often engages higher-order thinking skills and/or sensory input.
- Other benefits of reviewing content using movement include getting the benefit of a brain break (greater blood flow, etc.) without having to take one, engagement by all in the review process, an emotionally safe way to be involved with review, assessing students immediately with the right activity, and the possibility of anchoring a correct answer with a movement activity.
- Reviewing content in some form should happen on a consistent basis.
- Some activities may need to be altered to fit a specific grade level or content area.
- This chapter contains 20 review activities that incorporate movement including (1) Brain Snatch, (2) Challenge Flash Review, (3) Gallery Walk With Review Questions, (4) Body Webbing, (5) Square Dance

Discussion Circle, (6) The AP Line Jump, (7) Content Tag, (8) Human Transformations, (9) Five Signs Review, (10) Water Cycle Tag, (11) Vocabulary Review, (12) The Chaining Game, (13) Block Partners, (14) Relay Review, and (15) Word or Number Scramble Review.

TIPS FOR THE STAFF DEVELOPER

Teachers generally find these review activities very useful as they are engaging, energizing, community building, assessment oriented, and sometimes silent. Be sure to remind them that many of these activities can be altered to meet the needs of different age groups and content areas.

10

Teaching Content

⇨ Should I read and consider all the movement activities in this chapter, even if they are not in my content area?

⇨ What are eight movement activities that can be used to teach and learn language arts concepts?

⇨ What are eight movement activities that can be used to teach and learn math concepts?

⇨ What are eight movement activities that can be used to teach and learn science concepts?

⇨ What are eight movement activities that can be used to teach and learn social studies concepts?

⇨ What are two activities that can be used to teach and learn music concepts?

⇨ What are two activities that can be used to teach and learn art concepts?

⇨ What are two activities that can be used to teach and learn health concepts?

Using the body to learn is the epitome of the brain/body connection. When teaching content through kinesthetic activity, you can evoke the benefits of brain breaks, class cohesion, differentiating instruction, implicit learning, episodic memory, greater sensory engagement, and high levels of student engagement and motivation. Teachers will also find that students have greater recall because of the ease of learning through their bodies.

These activities are often the kinds that students can teach in homes the very evening they learned the concept at school. That's powerful for learning, retaining, recalling, and using school-related information. As you make decisions about lesson planning and curriculum, this is a concept that should be considered first. You might ask yourself, "Can I teach this academic concept through movement?" Sometimes the answer will be no, but you might be surprised how well movement lends itself to the teaching and learning process. In situations where you teach your standards though movement, you may not need or use the other purposes of movement on those particular days. This is your ultimate goal: to maximize efforts for winning the educational race and meeting academic objectives and goals through movement! In incidences where you are unable to think of methods for teaching your content through movement, the next step is to consider review activities with movement and your content. Your last consideration is to tap into the other purposes of movement that are not a direct connection between movement and content. It is our strong stance that this means of educational thinking and planning is a solid approach for increasing our speed in the race and reaching victorious moments regarding education success.

You might also consider activities that are not related to your content area by asking yourself, "Can this activity be used to teach information in my subject area?" Creative ideas will come more easily as you continue to design your activities and alter ones that are presented here. Teaching and learning through movement is an inventive resource well worth the time it takes to develop and perfect. Be patient with yourself, and allow a steady growth within your own comfort level. The attraction to movement for your students will be there; we just need to build your experience, comfort, and perspective of its necessity.

SHOULD I READ AND CONSIDER ALL THE MOVEMENT ACTIVITIES IN THIS CHAPTER, EVEN IF THEY ARE NOT IN MY CONTENT AREA?

Yes! You never know what information will trigger a creative thought. Education is cross curricular with a strong spiral profile. Reading through an activity not related to your field might inspire you to contemplate something you teach. Activities may need to be altered to fit your needs, but a number of ideas can originate from one activity. Many ideas and/or movement activities are often transferable. An activity used in science could match with information taught in English or social studies. Sometimes connections are made in the brain when we least expect it.

One of the goals of this chapter is to inspire your creative process about how your content can be taught through movement. The key is willingness to teach in a nontraditional manner. It can seem difficult at first, but know that it is expected. With patience, more ideas will come over time. As an expert in your subject area, and as you read about your content area in this chapter, allow your perspective to broaden as you consider everything you teach. With some thought and planning, you can build on these ideas and make them fit your needs. Continue to think about your students. By putting yourself in their shoes, you can imagine how it would feel when participating in the various activities. Once you see the increase in learning efficiency, you will be more motivated to expand the opportunities for teaching content through movement.

WHAT ARE EIGHT MOVEMENT ACTIVITIES THAT CAN BE USED TO TEACH AND LEARN LANGUAGE ARTS CONCEPTS?

LANGUAGE ARTS—Elementary

1. Word Hop—Phonics and word recognition
   - The classroom will become a book.
   - The teacher will spread letters and appropriate words in the room as if they would appear on the pages of a book.
   - Students will get in line and take turns hopping from left to right.
   - At the end of the line, they will walk over to the second row, go to the first letter or word, and begin to hop again. This will show how words have spaces between them as well as that reading occurs from left to right.
   - Students will continue hopping through the words as they continue down the page, showing we read from top to bottom.
   - When students finish hopping through the page, the teacher will discuss what happens next (turning the page).

2. Country Versus City: You Decide—Integration of knowledge and ideas
   - The teacher will have students use the entire classroom for the first part of the story. Mention the importance of good personal space.
   - When the teacher reads the part of the story (see passage that follows) about the country, the participants will act out whatever Bella sees. For the second part of the story, the teacher will use half the space (city) in the classroom while still insisting on safety and personal space. Students will again act out whatever Bella sees.
   - At the conclusion of the story, the instructor asks some questions to allow participants to analyze the story. (Where might you see chickens?)

- If student's answer is the country, he or she quickly walks around the entire room.
- If the answer is the city, the student goes to the side of the room, where the city was, and stands still.
- If the answer is country and city, students will go to the center of the room and lift their arms to the side while pointing to both sides of the room.
- At the conclusion of the activity, ask students where they would like to live and why.

Story

Hello, my name is Bella. My parents and I have a very big decision to make. My mom and dad said we have to move, and we need to choose between the city and the country. We decided to take a road trip to compare both places. My mom wants to live in the country. My dad wants to live in the city. I have no idea which place I would like better. I am hoping that seeing both places will help me decide.

We visited the county first. I saw some things that I thought were really cool. There were a lot of wide open spaces. I saw trees, ponds, and a lot of cool animals. Some of the animals I saw that I really liked were birds, cows, sheep, horses, cats, dogs, and deer. There were some things I didn't like in the county. There were a lot of bugs, bees, and flies. I even saw a snake that was very scary. My parents told me we were going to the city next, and I became excited about what I might see there.

The city had very tall buildings called skyscrapers. When I looked very closely, I saw them sway back and forth. I also saw a lot of people and noticed how crowded it was. There were some cool animals in the city too. I saw birds, cats, and dogs. I even saw a horse that was pulling a carriage filled with people. I didn't know there were horses in the city. There were some things in the city that I didn't like. There was garbage on some of the streets, and I even saw a rat. It was very big and looked mean. My mom told me there are rats in the country too.

Choosing to live in the city or the country is a very hard thing to do. They both have really cool things about them. They also have things about them that I didn't like. Lucky for me, my parents will probably make this decision. But, if they ask me, I don't know what I will say. Which would you pick?

3. The Syllable Slide—Phonological awareness
   - The teacher will discuss what a syllable is while demonstrating the syllable slide (slide sideways and clap for each syllable in a word).
   - The students will stand and practice the syllable slide with the following six words (or choose your own): country, bike, traveling, sunshine, friend, and tricycle.
   - The students will work with a partner to complete the handout (see a sample word list that follows).

○ The students will slide for the individual words as well as the words provided in the sentences.

○ Partners will then compare answers with a neighboring group.

4. Peer Editing Hop—Production and distribution of writing

○ Students will be given five to 10 minutes to write a short story on a regular size piece of paper.

○ When completed, students will spread their stories around the classroom floor—facedown.

○ Teacher will play music while students hop around the room (students are not allowed to hop on the stories). When the music stops, participants will hop near the closest story and pick it up.

○ Everyone will go back to their seats and begin to proofread the story.

○ The goal is for students to make one peer revision to the story they are reading.

○ Stories will then be spread around the room again, and the hopping will continue.

○ When the music goes off, students will find new stories, take them back to their seats, and again attempt to make one peer revision.

○ Continue the activity for several rounds.

○ Conclude the activity by students receiving their original stories and viewing the suggested corrections from their peers.

LANGUAGE ARTS—Secondary

5. Sentence Relay—Convention of standard English

○ Separate the class so that four people are on a team.

○ Have teams line up in the back of the room.

○ Place four signs on a table in the front of the room: simple, complex, compound, and compound-complex.

○ Give each team a color: blue, green, white, pink, and so on.

○ For the first race, each team will receive the same four sentences. The blue team's sentences will be on blue note cards, the green team's sentences on green cards, and so on.

○ When the teacher says, "Go," one person will speed walk to the front of the room to place his or her sentence under the correct sign. He or she will speed walk back and tag the next person. That person will take the next sentence up and place it under a sign.

○ Continue until everyone goes once.

○ Check to see if all groups agree, and share the correct answer.

○ Award a point to each team for each correctly labeled sentence.

○ Play three more rounds, each with four new sentences.

Review the following types of sentences:

a. Simple—contains a subject, verb, and complete thought

b. Compound—made up of two independent clauses connected to one another with a coordinating conjunction (for, and, nor, but, or, yet, or so)

c. Complex—made up of an independent clause and one or more dependent clauses connected to it

d. Compound-Complex—made from two independent clauses and one or more dependent clauses

6. The Fit Factor Decision—Comprehension and collaboration
   o Divide class into teams of two to five depending on the size of the class.
   o Give each group a notecard (list begins at Notecard 1, below).
   o Allow five to 10 minutes for groups to prepare their infomercials to promote the sale of a fitness program titled "The Fit Factor."
   o Each group will present its infomercial to the class. Inform participants to listen carefully to each presentation, as they will compare the information and data provided by each at the conclusion of the presentations.
   o After the presentations, students will answer the questions listed on p. 153.
   o Have students share answers while discussing the pros and cons of each infomercial.

Notecard 1
Design a two- to four-minute infomercial promoting the fitness program "The Fit Factor." The most important benefit of the program is weight loss. You want to make this point very clear. Some secondary benefits are increased cardiovascular endurance, muscle gain, and stress reduction. The program is a commitment of five days a week for 30 minutes each day, along with a strict nutritional guideline. You may create any information that is needed but not provided.
Cost = $99.99

Notecard 2
Design a two- to four-minute infomercial promoting the fitness program "The Fit Factor." The most important benefit of the program is increasing muscle mass. You want to make this point very clear. Some secondary benefits are increased cardiovascular endurance, weight loss, and stress reduction. The program is a commitment of five days a week for 30 minutes each day. You may create any information that is needed but not provided.
Cost = $99.99

Notecard 3
Design a two- to four-minute infomercial promoting the fitness program "The Fit Factor." The most important benefit of the program is enhancing self-esteem. You want to make this point very clear. Some secondary benefits are increased cardiovascular endurance, weight loss, and stress reduction. The program is a commitment of five days a week for 30 minutes each day, along

with a strict nutritional guideline. You may create any information that is needed but not provided.
Cost = $99.99

Notecard 4
Design a two- to four-minute infomercial promoting the fitness program "The Fit Factor." The most important benefit of the program is that it makes exercise fun. You want to make this point very clear. Some secondary benefits are increased cardiovascular endurance, weight loss, stress reduction, and muscle gain. The program is a commitment of five days a week for 30 minutes each day. You may create any information that is needed but not provided.
Cost = $99.99

Notecard 5 (needed only with larger classes)
Design a two- to four-minute infomercial promoting the fitness program "The Fit Factor." The most important benefit of the program is improving sleep patterns. You want to make this point very clear. Some secondary benefits are increased cardiovascular endurance, weight loss, stress reduction, and muscle gain. The program is a commitment of five days a week for 30 minutes each day, along with a strict nutritional guideline. You may create any information that is needed but not provided.
Cost = $99.99

Debrief: Have participants share and discuss the questions located in the course handouts.

Questions
Which infomercial was your favorite and why?
Which infomercial had the most impact on persuading you to purchase the program? Why?
Which infomercial did you find most informative?
Did you notice any discrepancies among the data provided in the presentations?

7. Transition Word Scramble—Text types and purposes
   o Separate the class into two to five teams depending on the size of the class.
   o Give each team a paragraph packet (making a peanut butter and jelly sandwich).
   o Teams will race to put their sentences in an appropriate order while writing and adding transition words to the blank note cards to make the paragraph flow.
   o At the end of the race, compare each group's paragraphs.
   o Continue with the second race while using another paragraph packet (the steps of the writing process).

Paragraph Packet 1: 32 note cards (16 blank for transition words or phrases—all cards must be used in the race)

a. To make a peanut butter and jelly sandwich, there are several steps to follow.
b. You take out the bread.
c. You take out the peanut butter and jelly.
d. You need to take out a knife and plate.
e. The bread is on the plate; you must open the peanut butter and jelly.
f. Put the knife in the peanut butter.
g. With the knife, smear the peanut butter on one slice of bread.
h. Place the knife in the sink.
i. Put the spoon in the jelly to scoop some out.
j. Smear the jelly on the top of the bread with the peanut butter.
k. Place the spoon in the sink.
l. Place the other piece of bread on the top of the bread with the peanut butter and jelly.
m. Put the lids on the jars, and put them back in the cabinet.
n. Close the bread bag and put it away.
o. Enjoy your sandwich.

Paragraph Packet 2: 22 notecards (11 blank for transition words or phrases—all cards must be used)

a. Brainstorm a list of ideas.
b. Create a web with one of your ideas.
c. Use an outline to further expand your thoughts.
d. Using your outline start drafting your outline.
e. Your draft is complete; you must revise your work.
f. Read over what you have written to make corrections.
g. Rearrange words or sentences to make them sound better.
h. You need to proofread your work by checking your grammar, spelling, and punctuation.
i. You have made your corrections; have someone else check your work.
j. You recopy your work correctly and neatly.
k. Present your paper to the class and the teacher.

8. Colon-Semi Fist Bump—Conventions of standard English
   ○ Have each student stand face-to-face with a partner.
   ○ Read a sentence containing a colon or semicolon.
   ○ Partners will use a double-knuckle fist bump (two fists in front of the body gently tapping the partner's fists) if they believe a colon should be used in the sentence or a double knuckle fist bump with a bottom fist swoop (two fists in front of the body gently tapping their partners fists, while the bottoms fists make a swoop-like movement) for a semicolon.

○ Partners will practice 10 sentences together by discussing which movement to use.

○ Then students will work alone by fist bumping the air while the teacher reads five more five sentences.

WHAT ARE EIGHT MOVEMENT ACTIVITIES THAT CAN BE USED TO TEACH AND LEARN MATH CONCEPTS?

MATH—Elementary

1. The Even/Odd Hop—Classifying numbers as even or odd
   ○ Using masking tape, create a line long enough for all students to line up on (front to back, not shoulder to shoulder).
   ○ After a quick review of even and odd numbers, call out numbers and have students hop to the left of the line for odds and to the right of the lines for evens.
   ○ If the number 0 is called, students should stand on the line because 0 is not considered to be even or odd.

2. Counting in Action—Learning to skip count
   ○ The class will stand and begin marching.
   ○ When the entire class is in step, prompt them to count together to 100.
   ○ While jogging in place count by twos to 100.
   ○ While hopping in place count by threes to 72.
   ○ While stepping side to side and back and forth—and clapping on each step—count by fives to 100.
   ○ Feel free to mix different physical activities with different number groupings, and begin with lower or higher than 72 or 100 according to age and ability.

3. Ascending and Descending Birthday—Learning ascending and descending order
   ○ Have all students write the date of their birthday (in large print) on a sheet of paper.
   ○ Ask all students to line up side by side, single file, in a large enough space in the room.
   ○ Tell students you would now like them to line up side by side but this time with the smallest number on the left side of the line and the largest number on right side.
   ○ All the students in between should line up according to their birthday number from smallest to largest in order.
   ○ Starting with the student on the left (whose birthday will most likely be the first, second, or third), have each student say their birthday number out loud, one by one from left to right.

○ Instruct the students that their birthday line, from smallest number to highest number, is said to be "ascending."
○ Repeat activity in reverse for descending order.

4. The Integer Dance—Learning how to add integers
   ○ Assign half of the students to represent positive signs and half to represent negative signs.
   ○ If you have an odd number of students, you can allow one student to choose his or her sign.
   ○ Students can either wear signs, sticky notes, or actually wear + or − signs made out of masking tape.
   ○ Jokingly instruct the participants to line up on two sides of the room, negatives on one side and positives on the other, as if this were the first middle school dance and students were too nervous to socialize with each other.
   ○ Start playing upbeat music, and instruct the students to find a partner—pairs must consist of one negative and one positive.
   ○ Once everyone has a partner, have them discuss the overall value of each pair—which happens to be zero. Once this idea has been solidified, have students split back into their original two groups of positives and negatives.
   ○ Display the problem 3 + (−2) on the board, and have three "positive" students come out onto the "dance floor" along with two "negative" students.
   ○ Students should pair up with opposite signs to create "zero pairs."
   ○ Any students left without a partner represent the final answer.
   ○ For example, with the problem 3 + (−2), two positives and two negatives create two zero pairs, with one positive left over. Therefore, the answer is 1.
   ○ Have students return to their original groups of positives and negatives, then follow up with additional problems, until you feel students have had adequate practice and understand the concept.

MATH—Secondary

5. Human Box-and-Whiskers Plots—Practicing estimation skills while kinesthetically modeling box-and-whisker plots
   ○ Prompt the students for an estimate of some sort. One engaging example might be: "Estimate the number of hours that a cockroach can survive without its head."
   ○ Instruct students to make their estimates silently, and record their answers on sticky notes or mini whiteboards. Then have students arrange themselves in a line from smallest estimate to largest estimate.

- You may want to allow students a few moments to discuss why they gave the answers they did.
- As a class, determine which students represent the "minimum" and "maximum" data points.
- Distribute the correct signs to those students, and have them hold them until the end of the activity.
- Next, figure out which student represents the "median." If you have an odd number of students in line, this will be the student standing in the middle. If you have an even number of students in line, the two middle students will hold this sign between them.
- Finally, determine which students represent the "lower quartile" (the median of the lower half of the data) and the "upper quartile" (the median of the upper half of the data), and have them hold the appropriate signs.
- Last, have the students holding the "minimum" and "lower quartile" signs hold onto the ends of one of the sections of rope, and the students holding the "maximum" and "upper quartile" signs hold onto the ends of the other section of rope.
- Repeat the activity a few times with other estimation prompts so that students take turns standing at different places in the line and engage in repeated practice with the terms.

6. Destroyer: Systems of Equations Review—Visualizing the solution to a system of equations and testing the solutions kinesthetically (please see the related worksheet on pp. 158–159)
    - If there is adequate room on the classroom floor, or if students can be taken outside, prepare a grid on the floor using tape or sidewalk chalk. If you do not have adequate floor space, the grid can be created on large poster paper and hung on the wall or chalkboard.
    - The x- and y-axes should range from –20 to 20. The teacher is assigned three linear equations that represent the pats of his or her "battleships."
    - Split students into teams of two to four students, and give each team of students one additional linear equation and three sticky dots.
    - The students are to determine the points where their equations will intersect the teacher's equations (battleship paths) and place sticky dots on the grid at those (x,y) coordinates.
    - Each of the students' lines will intersect each teacher's line at one point.
    - When all students' points are placed, use a string or rope to plot the teacher's equation, and see how many of the students' points intersected the teacher's "battleship path" correctly.
    - Teams get points for each target that was correctly placed.

BATTLESHIPS SYSTEMS OF EQUATIONS REVIEW

Name: _____

Problem Statement

You are navigating a battleship during war games. Your course will take you across several enemy shipping lanes. Your mission is to lay mines at the points where your course crosses the enemy lanes. The enemy shipping lanes are represented by the following equations:

Enemy Lane 1: $x - y = -4$

Enemy Lane 2: $3x - y = 10$

Enemy Lane 3: $x - 2y = -2$

The teacher will assign your group an equation. Determine the points where your equation (the path of your battleship) will intersect each of the enemy shipping lanes. Use any of the methods discussed in the text for solving a system of equations. Round your answers to the nearest 0.1 unit before they are recorded.

Points of Intersection

Enemy Lane	xy-coordinates
1	
2	
3	

Cut out three 1-inch squares of colored paper. Each square represents a "mine" dropped by your battleship. Each group should use a different color.

For each point of intersection, locate the corresponding point on the classroom floor. Use masking tape to fasten a piece of colored paper to the floor at each point of intersection. This will indicate where your battleship has dropped a "mine."

After all the groups have completed "dropping their mines," we will check each group's success. The equations for the shipping lanes are linear and represent lines. Find two ordered pairs on each of these three lines.

Ordered Pairs on Enemy Lanes

Enemy Lane	Ordered Pair #1 (x,y)	Ordered Pair #2 (x,y)
1		
2		
3		

As a class, we will use a string to connect the ordered pairs for each line. These three strings represent the three enemy shipping lanes. **Did your "mines" lie within the shipping lanes?**

Equations for Groups' Battleships

Equation 1: $5x + 4y = 48$

Equation 2: $x + y = 18$

Equation 3: $3x + y = 10$

Equation 4: $15x - 200y = -1800$

Equation 5: $9x + 5y = 180$

Equation 6: $-x + 5y = 25$

Equation 7: $12x + 8y = 128$

Equation 8: $100x + 400y = 5200$

7. Simon Says, Parent Graph Edition—Demonstrating the shapes of parent graphs
   o Directions are the same as in the children's game Simon Says.
   o All students stand, and the teacher asks the students to model the shape of a parent graph (line, parabola, cubic, absolute value, square root, exponential, hyperbola, logarithm, sine, cosine, etc.).
   o If the teacher says "Simon Says" before calling out a type of graph, students are to model the shape of the graph with their bodies.
   o All students who do not make a graph, or who model the incorrect graph, must sit down.
   o If the teacher does not say "Simon Says" before calling out a type of graph, any students making a graph must sit down.

8. People Graphing—Observing the effect of performing an operation on an input value and recording the output value on a graph
   o If outdoors, prepare a large grid on the ground, going from –15 to 15 on the x-axis, and –15 to 15 on the y-axis.
   o If indoors, prepare a graph on grid poster paper with the same coordinates, and hang it on the chalkboard. Pass out the index cards to the students in the class.
   o There will probably be more students than there are cards. This is OK because the students can take turns participating in each round.
   o The cards represent the x-coordinates of points that will be plotted.
   o If outdoors, students form a horizontal line while standing on the x-coordinate that matches their card.
   o If indoors, have magnets located in a horizontal line on each of the x-coordinates.
   o Direct students to perform an operation (or multiple operations) on the number on their index card, and then move themselves (or the proper magnet) forward or backward, staying in their assigned "x lane," to the correct y-coordinate.
   o Students can keep track of the shapes of the graphs on a worksheet that accompanies the problems.
   o This is a great activity that enforces the proper locations of the x- and y-coordinates. It can be used for a variety of graphing skills, ranging from introductory plotting of points to graphing more difficult functions.

   Sample Equations (and verbal commands given by the teacher to direct students how to move):
   $y = x + 3$ ("add 3 to your number")
   $y = 10 - x$ ("subtract your number from 10")
   $y = 2x$ ("double your number")
   $y = \frac{1}{2}x - 1$ ("take half of your number and subtract 1")

y = x^2 ("multiply your number by itself")
y = |x| ("find the absolute value of your number")

WHAT ARE EIGHT MOVEMENT ACTIVITIES THAT CAN BE USED TO TEACH AND LEARN SCIENCE CONCEPTS?

SCIENCE—Elementary

1. Biomes—Learning about biomes
   - Place five signs around the room with different biomes listed (aquatic, forest, tundra, dessert, and forest).
   - Scatter note cards around the room containing definitions and descriptions of each biome (include pictures if you'd like).
   - Have students mill around the room by themselves or with a partner.
   - They pick up one card at a time to try and match it to the biome by sticking it on the wall at the correct place. Any student can move a card if he or she doesn't agree.
   - Reflect and review correct answers.
   - You can add a review game where you read the cards and students go to the correct biomes.

2. Magnet Tag—Experiencing magnetic force
   - Discuss polarity, and make the human body north (front) and south (back) poles.
   - All students are magnets.
   - Discuss repel and unite.
   - Choose someone to be "it."
   - This person can tag anyone who is not linked to another player.
   - Players can link north and south poles to be safe for five seconds, then they must repel.
   - If the "it" person tags someone, that person is now "it."
   - Repeat the game as needed!

3. Conduction, Convection, Ra-Ra Radiation—Demonstrating the three methods that heat energy can be transferred to and from.
   - Students will say the cheer: "Conduction! Convection! Raaaadiation!"
   - Conduction occurs when an object touches the heat source, and the heat energy moves through it.
   - Convection occurs when a current is created due to differences in density and temperature. (I would highly suggest doing this activity after students understand the difference between the densities of hot air vs. cold air.)

○ Radiation occurs as heat being given off where no medium is required for it to travel.

Movements
a. Conduction: press fingers together, representing the need to touch the heat source
b. Convection: make large arm circles, creating an up-and-down effect and moving large quantities of air
c. Radiation: holding a hand up in front of you as if you were sitting in front of a nice, hot fire

4. Density—Demonstrating what determines an object's density
○ Place Hula Hoops around the room (or in a designated area).
○ Play a song, and when the music stops, have the students go into a Hula Hoop.
○ Once in the Hula Hoop, have the students count how many of them are in the ring and write these values on the board.
○ Assuming that the Hula Hoops are all the same size, have the students determine which is now the most densely packed (the most students per Hula Hoop).
○ Using something larger in area than the Hula Hoops (e.g., larger Hula Hoops, rope, string, or chalk). Make the same number of locations as you had for the original Hula Hoops (repeat the activity). Show how, if you increase the area but have the same number of people in the area as the smaller area, you will have a lower density. You can also make smaller circles to show higher density.

SCIENCE—Secondary

5. Human Diffusion—Showing how gases flow
○ Have all students roll their dice to fill in the 40 "turns" (see worksheet on p. 164).
○ Take the students outside, where you draw a square on the ground for all of them to stand in.
○ The students should have a piece of graph paper with a square drawn on it (everyone should have the same size square).
○ Have the students stand in the square and make a mark in their square representing where they are standing. All students should also identify the same building on their sheets (write "school," etc.).
○ Go through each step marking each of their moves; they do not need to mark a spot again if they end up in it more than once.
○ Once finished with all of the steps, go back to the classroom, have the students gather in lab groups, and transfer their dots onto overhead sheets using permanent marker.

- Then overlay the graphs on each other to show the diffusion of the gases.
- One idea to focus on is that gases can travel all around and that they can go back into a container.
- You can also discuss how molecules collide with each other, and despite the fact that the average speed of a gas molecule is 1,150 miles per hour, it takes a significant amount of time for a gas (like an air freshener) to travel through a room.
- Further discussion: discuss how changing the temperature would affect the speed of movement of the gases.
- Tie this information to gases in the atmosphere.

HUMAN DIFFUSION OF GASES LAB WORKSHEET

Name _____

Directions: You must complete 40 rounds of dice rolling. For each roll of the die, record the outcome in the space provided. Do not record the number rolled. DO record the word that corresponds to the outcome as follows:

1: Front 2: Right 3: Back 4: Left 5: Wait (If you roll a 6 you must roll again until you get anything from 1–5.)	
1.	21.
2.	22.
3.	23.
4.	24.
5.	25.
6.	26.
7.	27.
8.	28.
9.	29.
10.	30.
11.	31.
12.	32.
13.	33.
14.	34.
15.	35.
16.	36.
17.	37.
18.	38.
19.	39.
20.	40.

6. Electricity: That's How It Flows—Understanding electricity and how it flows
   ○ Explain that each student is an atom.
   ○ Divide the class in to two groups, and have them stand in a haphazard line (they do not need to be shoulder to shoulder, showing that in a wire, the atoms aren't all exactly in a straight line) holding an "electron" (use a marker, pencil, ball, or anything you can have many of).
   ○ At the end of each row, put a pile of extra electrons (electricity) and a person to feed them to the wire. This will represent the generator.
   ○ Explain that the movement of electrons through the wire is called the current or amperage (amp). The speed at wish they travel through the wire is called the voltage.
   ○ When the instructor says "power on," the participants will begin to move their electrons down the wire, putting them in a box at the end.
   ○ They do not need to pass the projects to each person in the row, but they cannot jump over someone next to them.
   ○ The box will represent the object being powered (feel free to decorate the box to look like an object powered by electricity—a TV, iPod, etc.).
   ○ The line that gets the electrons to the end first had the higher voltage.

7. Mole Conversion Activity/Physical Phenceposting—Having students convert information to solve a problem and to physically create the equation (see worksheet on p. 166)
   ○ Each student will be given a worksheet with each problem, so they can reference it and attempt the work themselves.
   ○ Divide the students into six groups.
   ○ Each group will be assigned one of the problems from the worksheet along with all possible conversion data. The group will determine the correct way to set up the problem then display it to the class.
   ○ Set up four chairs.
   ○ The student holding the starting information stands on the first chair.
   ○ On the second and subsequent chairs, students will stand on the chair representing the information needed to convert units.
   ○ Each group will not need to use all four chairs.

PHYSICAL PHENCEPOSTING WORKSHEET

Name _____

1. Nitrous oxide (N_2O) is a colorless gas commonly known as laughing gas. N_2O is also a major component to greenhouse gases, and it has almost 300 times greater impact on the environment than carbon dioxide. If an aerosol manufacturer produced 0.50 grams of N_2O in every bottle of hair spray, how many moles did they produce?

2. A chemical company producing chlorine gas (Cl_2 also known as mustard gas) during World War I produced 500 grams of Cl_2 gas during a shift. How many moles of the gas were produced?

3. At the Macy's Thanksgiving Day parade, balloons are going to be filled with helium (He) gas. If it takes 20,000 grams of He to fill Garfield, how many atoms of He are in him?

4. Humans exhale approximately 1,000 grams of carbon dioxide (CO_2) every day. How many molecules does a person exhale every day?

5. Plasma televisions use neon (Ne) gas inside of them. If they were to use 1.0 mole of neon gas, how much mass would that add to the television?

6. When pumping new hydrogen (H) gas at the gas station, a customer used 7.23 x 1023 molecules of gas. How many grams was it?

8. The Body Systems—Learning the body systems

Teach the following body systems with the movements described:
- ○ Skeletal—stand in the anatomical position of a skeleton
- ○ Digestive—put fingers up to your mouth and act like you are chewing, then rub belly and say "mmm"
- ○ Muscular—make muscles and kiss your biceps
- ○ Respiratory—breathe in and out
- ○ Circulatory—beat on your chest like a heart, then shake the body to show blood being pumped around.

WHAT ARE EIGHT MOVEMENT ACTIVITIES THAT CAN BE USED TO TEACH AND LEARN SOCIAL STUDIES CONCEPTS?

SOCIAL STUDIES—Elementary

1. Money and Making a Dollar—Learning economics
   - ○ Each group will receive a packet of 3 × 5 cards with the following denominations on them: 10 pennies, 10 nickels, 10 dimes, four quarters; blank pieces of paper; and markers.
   - ○ Ask the class, "What is money?" Money is anything widely accepted as final payment for goods and services.
   - ○ Review the denominations of money with the class.
   - ○ Show them real coins, and they must use their fingers to show the denominations (for a quarter they have two fingers in one hand and five in the other to signify 25 cents).
   - ○ Next, break the class into groups of six to eight.
   - ○ Have each group create a "batting order" from 1 to as many are in their group.
   - ○ Give each group three to five minutes to create as many possible combinations of $1 as they can.
   - ○ The first "batter" arranges the group into a unique $1 single-file line. Coins used are recorded.
   - ○ Students must physically arrange themselves in a single file line before they are allowed to record their score.
   - ○ If a person cannot find a unique arrangement, he or she can use a previous arrangement as long as they do not look at the record sheet.

2. Marketing, Bartering, and Negotiating—Learning economics (continuation of Money and Making a Dollar)
   - ○ Each group should have $2.60 cents worth of currency.
   - ○ Each group will be given five blank pieces of paper.
   - ○ Instruct each group to choose a business they would like to specialize in that creates a product or performs a service or

leisure activity. You have the option to allow repeat businesses to demonstrate competition, or you can request that the business remain unique to show the interdependence of specialized businesses.
- On the blank pieces of paper, groups must draw and label five items they think the rest of the class would want.
- All items priced must be less than $2 but could be valued much greater. You are allowed to resell items acquired from other groups. Ask the class for examples.
- Explain the concepts of "bartering" and "negotiating."
- Once a deal is made, a handshake is the receipt of trade, and all deals are final.
- Each group will select shoppers and storekeepers. The shoppers and storekeepers are trying to get the best deals possible.
- When all of the groups are ready, open the market.

Debrief
- Ask the class who ended up with the greatest amount of money.
- Which group thinks they got the best deal on goods and services?
- What was the hardest part of negotiations? Explain the concept of "scarcity."

3. The Human Map—Understanding global mapping and population distribution
   - Have one cone available for each of the seven continents and place it as a marker for each continent: North and South America, Africa, Asia, Europe, Australia, and Antarctica.
   - Have the students form a rectangle facing in around the continents.
   - Have the class repeat the name of the continent as you point to it.
   - Ask the class to brainstorm the following: "if this map represented the world population, and each of you equally divided the world's 7+ billion people (http://www.census.gov/popclock/), where would you end up?" Give the class one minute to divide their numbers by seven and figure out where each person should go.

Answers: (2011) Wikipedia—	Class of 30	Class of 20
Asia—4,140,336,501 60%	(18)	(12)
Africa—994,527,534 14%	(4)	(3)
Europe—738,523,843 11%	(3)	(2)
North America—528,720,588 7.5%	(2.5)	(1.5)
South America—385,742,554 5.5%	(2)	(1.5)
Australia—36,102,071 0.04%	(.5)	(0)
Antarctica—4,900 (non-permanent, varies) 0.00007% (0%)	(0)	

4. Hands Across America—Using maps and mental maps to organize information in a spatial context
   ○ Have the students review a map of the United States.
   ○ Have them take note of each state and its location in relation with other states.
   ○ One student starts by calling out a state—someone must join hands with him or her by calling out a state that is connected (by border) and holding hands. The next person must connect to either the first state or the last state connected (use a map for reference).

SOCIAL STUDIES—Secondary

Note: The secondary social studies section of this chapter is treated with more depth and is formatted a bit differently. Read each activity (lesson) thoroughly before implementation. The time for each activity could vary greatly.

5. Trench Warfare—Learning about trench warfare during World War I

   Part 1—Gallery Walk
   ○ Have students take a *gallery walk* around the classroom looking at pictures of the following (all can be found on Wikipedia or Google images):
     a. Different trench constructions
     b. Diagrams of trenches
     c. Soldiers in trenches
     d. Rats
     e. Gangrene
     f. Pre-packaged meals
     g. Poor sanitary conditions—dysentery, typhus, cholera
     h. Trench foot—trench mouth
     i. Map of the opposing countries in the conflict—the Allied Powers versus the Central Powers
     j. Frostbite
   ○ Have the class discuss what they saw, what they thought about the soldiers' lives, and any questions they might have.

   Part 2—Division of Powers
   ○ Divide the class into two sides.
   ○ Identify the warring countries:

   The Allied Powers—British Empire, Americans, and Russians (BAR) represented by holding up three fingers: pointer, middle, and ring

Versus

The Central Powers—the German empire, the Austro-Hungarian empire, and the kingdom of Bulgaria (GAB) represented by holding up three fingers: thumb, pointer, and middle finger

Part 3—Planning and Replanning

○ Give students two minutes to set up munitions (paper balls) and trenches (tables, chairs, stacks of books, etc.).

○ After time is called, have them look at their opponent's fortifications and give them one more minute to make any final adjustments to their side.

○ Make sure to establish a "no man's land" in the middle of the classroom.

Part 4—Get Your Medics Ready

○ Identify the medical officer for each side (have them draw the Red Cross symbol on a piece of paper). They are allowed to walk an injured soldier to one of their team's "medical tents" located in the four corners of the classroom. It was common practice during World War I to have a cease-fire during the battle to allow the Red Cross to remove injured soldiers from battle.

○ At the medical tents center, there are different "rehabilitation" exercises that can be done to get the soldier healthy enough to return to battle. Pre-packaged meals—represented by small foam balls—are placed in "no man's land" (the area between the two opposing armies).

○ Have signs printed on a piece of paper in the four corners of the classroom:

Red Cross Medical Tent (print on four pieces of paper, and post in all four corners of the classroom—two on each side of each trench)

Rehab Exercises

a. Rat Bites—10 jumping Jacks

b. Gangrene—10 push-ups or modified push-ups

c. Dysentery, Typhus, or Cholera—10 crunches

d. Trench Foot—run in place for 40 steps

e. Trench Mouth—10 snapping turtles (jump into the air like you are biting at some food overhead)

f. Frostbite—10 air squats

g. Gunshot Wound—10 cross lateral hops

h. Rifle Wound—10-second Superman

Pre-packaged meals can be used to replace any of the exercises and return you to battle.

Part 5—Let the War Begin

○ To signal the start of the battle, play war noises: http://www.youtube.com/watch?v=hS3x-XMm89E.

○ When you say freeze: Each team will have to answer a question (either writing it down on a piece of paper or dry erase board). If they get it correct, they gain another pre-packaged meal (a foam ball); if they answer incorrectly, they get sent to rehab with a shrapnel wound.

Possible Questions
○ List your team's name: Central or Allied Powers
○ List all of the major countries your team represents: either BAR (British Empire, Americans, and the Russians) or the GAB (German empire, the Austro-Hungarian empire, and the kingdom of Bulgaria)
○ List all of the opposite team's countries: the opposite answer to number 2
○ What year did World War I officially begin?: 1914
○ How did the United States get involved?
○ What year did the war end?: 1918 (with this question you can end the battle)
○ Periodically attribute different ailments to the troops (mix them in with the questions).

Possible Ailments
○ All the soldiers wearing grey shirts, you have just received a rat bite—seek medical help.
○ All the soldiers who are left-handed, you have gangrene on your foot and leg—seek medical help.
○ All the soldiers who are wearing black shoes, you have dysentery, typhus, or cholera—seek medical help.
○ All the soldiers wearing socks colored other than white, you have trench foot—seek medical help.
○ All of the soldiers who have blond hair, you have trench mouth—seek medical help.
○ All of the soldiers who are wearing a ring, you have frostbite—seek medical help.
○ End the war—debrief the soldiers' experience. Have the class understand that the casualty rate was 55 percent (dead or injured)—10 percent dead.

6. The American Industrial Revolution

Part 1—Paint the Picture
○ The year is 1812. . . . The United States has just finished the battle for independence, started more than 25 years ago, from the British. It's a growing nation with many needs, and local manufacturing is not keeping up with the demand.
○ Question: "What were the three things that were needed for the Industrial Revolution?": transportation (roads, canals, railroads),

power (hydro, steam, electricity for machines and light), and improvements in refining processes (metals).

○ "Let's see if it really makes sense in a practical application."

Part 2—Manufacturing by Localized Independent Businesses

○ Everyone take out a piece of paper.

○ You are all now professional paper airplane manufacturers before the Industrial Revolution. You provide all of the paper airplane needs for your small community in Yourtown, USA.

Follow the basic design idea (see Figure 10.1):

a. Midline fold—Fold the paper in half.

b. Right cockpit fold—Fold the top right corner into the midline crease.

c. Left cockpit fold—Fold the top left corner into the midline crease.

d. Right hull fold—Fold the right side of the paper on an angle from the top midline crease to the bottom right corner.

e. Left hull fold—Fold the left side of the paper on an angle from the top midline crease to the bottom left corner.

f. Whole plane fold—Fold both halves using the midline fold.

g. Right wing fold—With the plane lying on its left side, fold the wing one inch from the bottom straight across, leaving about one inch of hull.

Figure 10.1   Standardized Folding Instructions

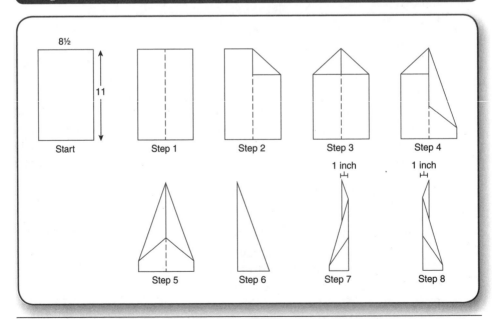

Source: Original art by Phillip Hochman.

h. Left wing fold—With the plane lying on its left side, fold the wing one inch from the bottom straight across, leaving about one inch of hull.

Part 3—Let the Revolution Begin
○ Break the class into two teams.
○ Let them know that one group of workers thinks their production strategy of "everyone for themselves" is the best idea.
○ The other group likes the "production line strategy."
○ Give each group some time to practice their craft.
○ Then see how many they can produce in two minutes. Let the teams switch to see if it was just the individuals on the team.

Part 4—Debrief
○ Debrief the differences and the cost-benefit ratio of using the production line versus the individual small business.

7. The Plague (14th to 17th centuries)

Materials
Find pictures of the following:
○ China
○ Ilkhanate (modern-day Iran, Pakistan, and Afghanistan)
○ Khanate (modern-day Turkey and Southwest Russia)
○ France
○ Castile (modern-day Spain)
○ Holy Roman Empire (modern-day Germany, Austria, and Hungary)
○ England
○ India
○ The kingdom of Poland
○ Ghazi Emirates (modern-day Turkey)
○ Naples and Sicily (modern-day Italy)
○ Egypt
   Background—Originally thought to have originated in China, the *Yersinia pestis* bacterium traveled on rat fleas on merchant ships and through the Silk Road to Europe, killing between 75 and 200 million people. Total world population at that time is estimated at 450 million people.
   Additional materials: Country signs (with their geographical location) 10 pipe cleaners per country, one cone per country, one 3 × 5 card per group (12 groups total) with the following instructions on them:
○ **China**—They want to trade with everyone but are limited in their reach and can trade directly only with India, the Ilkhanate, and the Khanate via land routes. They can go directly to Turkey and Egypt via land routes. They want to gain gold and silver. (China starts with 10 red and 10 black pipe cleaners representing silk and

spices.) Create a trade agreement using the Ghazi Emirates and Ilkhanate to trade with the rest of Europe.

- **Ilkhanate** (modern-day Iran, Pakistan, and Afghanistan)—They serve as the middleman for much of the land trade from and to China. Trade is heavy with India and the Ghazi Emirates, but they rarely trade beyond that. They do not trade with Poland. They wants a mix of gold and silver and spices. (Ilkhanate starts with five yellow and white pipe cleaners representing gold and silver and five red and black pipe cleaners five representing spices and silk.)

- **Khanate** (modern-day Turkey and Southwest Russia)—Centrally located there is heavy trade with India, China, Egypt, Ghazi Emirates, and the Holy Roman Empire. They do not trade with Poland. They want a mix of gold and silver and spices. (Khanate starts with five yellow and five white pipe cleaners representing gold and silver and five red and five black pipe cleaners representing spices and silk.)

- **France**—With a strong navy, they have ships going to England, China, and India along with land trade with Spain, the Holy Roman Empire, and Italy. They do not trade with Poland. They want silk and spices. (France gets 10 white and 10 yellow pipe cleaners representing gold and silver.)

- **Castile** (modern-day Spain)—With a strong navy they have ships going to England, China, and India along with land trade with France, the Holy Roman Empire, Naples and Sicily, and the Ghazi Emirates. They want silk and spices. (Castile gets 10 white and 10 yellow pipe cleaners representing gold and silver.)

- **Holy Roman Empire** (modern-day Germany, Austria, and Hungary)—A centrally located European nation, they have trade with France, Spain, England (via ships), Naples and Sicily, Ghazi Emirates, Ilkhanate, Khanate, and Egypt. They have very limited trade with Poland. They want silk and spices. (The Holy Roman Empire gets 10 white and 10 yellow pipe cleaners representing gold and silver.)

- **England**—One of the farthest countries but one of the wealthiest, they demand much of the spice and silk. Because they are on an island, they have ships traveling around Africa to India and China. Along with ships to France and Spain, trading occurs with the Holy Roman Empire and Naples and Sicily. They do not trade with Poland. They want silk and spices. (England gets 10 white and 10 yellow pipe cleaners representing gold and silver.)

- **India**—Exporting spices as well, India has strong trade with China, Ilkhanate, Khanate, Naples and Sicily, Ghazi Emirates, and Egypt. (India gets 10 red pipe cleaners to represent spices.)

- **The kingdom of Poland**—Desiring trade, but not being the wealthiest country, trade is limited with all other countries.

(Poland gets 10 blue pipe cleaners to represent crops.) They attempt trade with all countries.

- **Ghazi Emirates** (modern-day Turkey)—A centrally located country that bridges the land route for the Silk Road. This nation acts in many ways as a middleman for transporting goods from west to east and vice versa. They do not trade with Poland. Decide whether or not to increase silk, spices, gold, or silver, and stick with that decision. (Ghazi Emirates receives five yellow and five white pipe cleaners representing gold and silver and five red and five black pipe cleaners representing spices and silk.)
- **Naples and Sicily** (modern-day Italy)—A very popular sea destination for trade with India and China (over land through Egypt) and a heavy trader with the Ghazi Emirates, the Holy Roman Empire, Spain, France, and England. They do not trade with Poland. Decide whether or not to increase silk, spices, gold, or silver, and stick with that decision. (Naples and Sicily receive five yellow and five white pipe cleaners representing gold and silver and five red and five black pipe cleaners representing spices and silk.)
- **Egypt**—A popular land destination for trade with India, China, and Hungary. They also have land routes with the Ghazi empire. They do not trade with Poland. Decide whether or not to increase silk, spices, gold, or silver, and stick with that decision. (Egypt receives five yellow and five white pipe cleaners representing gold and silver and five red and five black pipe cleaners representing spices and silk.)
- **Hungary**—A centrally located European nation, they have trade with France, Castile, the Holy Roman Empire, Naples and Sicily, Ghazi Emirates, Ilkhanate, Khanate, and Egypt. They have very limited trade with Poland. They want gold and silver. (Hungary receives five yellow and five white pipe cleaners representing gold and silver and five red and five black pipe cleaners representing spices and silk.)

Part 1—Jigsaw Puzzle the 14th Century
- Distribute pipe cleaners to the countries:
  a. white pipe cleaners representing silver
  b. yellow pipe cleaners representing gold
  c. blue pipe cleaners representing crops
  d. red pipe cleaners representing spices
  e. black pipe cleaners representing silk
- Once everyone has their country sign, their 3 × 5 card, and pipe cleaners, post the map on a PowerPoint slide.
- Mark the room's walls north, south, east, and west. Have them get into their geographical locations.
- Once a group thinks they are in the correct location, they should put their cone on the ground and sit next to it.

○ They can use the picture on the overhead to organize themselves like a jigsaw puzzle. Once everyone is in the correct position, begin step 2.

Part 2—An Economy of Trade
○ Option 1: Start out with China, and work your way west.
○ Go one country at a time, and have them trade for 90 seconds.
○ Explain that they want to make the best deal possible. They do not have to trade the pipe cleaners one for one; they could hold out for a better deal.
○ Option 2: Have all of the countries trading at the same time.

Part 3—Debrief
○ After all of the countries have a chance to trade, ask who thinks they made the best deals. Then reveal that if they have a black or red pipe cleaner, their country was infected with the plague. Discuss the impact across Europe; mention that Poland remained mostly uneffected.

8. Unhappy Baseball

Materials: four Hula Hoops, one inflatable beach ball, and one cone
○ Explain to students that they are going to relive an era in American history but are not going to be told which era.
○ They are also going to play a classic American sport, modified for indoors.
○ Have the class understand that although there are a clear set of rules, they will not all be shared.
○ Break the class up into two teams: males and females.
○ Give the rules of the game: three outs then switch the batting team; the Hula Hoops will count as different base hits: first hoop is a single, second hoop a double, third hoop a triple, and the fourth hoop a home run.
Unwritten rule: When calling the player out, DO NOT explain why, have them figure it out.
For Girls:
○ Three fouls (the ball not landing in the hoop) is an out.
○ Anyone stepping past the first cone is warned silently by the teacher.
○ Girls can arbitrarily be called safe because of "errors" on the other team, such as "balks," "dropped fly balls," etc.
For Boys:
○ One foul is an out.
○ Throwing overhand is an automatic out.
○ Bouncing the ball is an automatic out.
○ Anyone stepping past the first cone is automatically out.
○ Any arguing of a call is an automatic "extra" out (can be applied to the next inning if it occurs during the girls' at bat).

Game

○ Have the class play three to five innings (depending on how fast the boys get out) of the game, and debrief their experience.

Post game

Ask the class:

○ How did they feel during the experience?

○ For the girls: Would you like to play more of this sport? Could you see yourself unwilling to make changes to the "unwritten rules"?

○ For the boys: What emotions did you experience? How could this affect your life if the deck was stacked like this all day, every day?

○ Ask the class: From what decade do you think we were reversing the discrimination?

Explain that the roles of females in America were narrowed to being a housewife. Trying to argue got you out, which was like differing from the norms of the time. Working outside the house, having children outside of wedlock, or getting divorced got you ostracized from many communities. Trying new or innovative ideas got you mocked, laughed at, and out. Trying to pass boundaries set by society, such as wearing certain clothing or being seen with different cultures, classes, or races got you out. You were limited in the amount of times you could try and fail (one foul and you are out compared to three fouls for males).

So what has happened?

1961

President John Kennedy establishes the President's Commission on the Status of Women to explore issues relating to women and to make proposals in areas such as employment policy, education, and federal Social Security and tax laws relating to women. Kennedy appointed Eleanor Roosevelt, former U.S. delegate to the United Nations and widow of President Franklin D. Roosevelt, to chair the commission. The report issued by the commission in 1963 documents substantial discrimination against women in the workplace and makes specific recommendations for improvement, including fair hiring practices, paid maternity leave, and affordable child care.

How would that change our game?

1963

Betty Friedan publishes her highly influential book *The Feminine Mystique,* which describes the dissatisfaction felt by middle-class American housewives with the narrow role imposed on them by society. The book immediately becomes a best seller.

According to *The New York Times* obituary of Friedan (Fox, 2006), it "ignited the contemporary women's movement in 1963 and as a result permanently transformed the social fabric of the United States and countries around the world" and "is widely regarded as one of the most influential nonfiction books of the 20th century."

How would that change our game?

Congress passes the Equal Pay Act, an amendment to the Fair Labor Standards Act of 1938, requiring employers to pay all employees equally for equal work, regardless of gender. The act prohibits unequal pay for equal or substantially equal work performed by men and women in the same establishment who are performing under similar working conditions.

How would that change our game?

1966
National Organization for Women (NOW) is formed by a group of feminists including Betty Friedan while attending the Third National Conference of Commissions on the Status of Women. It becomes the largest women's rights group in the United States and begins working to end sexual discrimination, especially in the workplace, by means of legislative lobbying, litigation, and public demonstrations.

How would that change our game?

1967
Executive Order 11375 (amending Executive Order 11246) expands President Lyndon Johnson's affirmative action policy of 1965 to cover discrimination based on gender. As a result, federal agencies and contractors must take active measures to ensure that women as well as minorities enjoy the same educational and employment opportunities as white males.

How would that change our game?

1968
The Equal Employment Opportunity Commission issues revised guidelines on sex discrimination, making it clear that the widespread practice of publishing "help wanted" advertisements that use "male" and "female" column headings violates Title VII. This ruling is upheld in 1973 by the Supreme Court and opens the way for women to apply for higher-paying jobs hitherto open only to men.

How would that change our game?

1972
Congress sends the proposed Equal Rights Amendment (ERA) to the Constitution to the states for ratification. Originally drafted by Alice Paul in 1923, the amendment reads: "Equality of rights under the law shall not be denied or abridged by the United States or by any State on account of sex." Congress places a seven-year deadline on the ratification process, and although the deadline extends until 1982, the amendment does not receive enough state ratifications. It is still not part of the U.S. Constitution.

How would that change our game?

1972
Title IX of the Education Amendments bans sex discrimination in schools. It states: "No person in the United States shall, on the basis of sex, be excluded from participation in, be denied the benefits of, or be subjected to discrimination under any educational program or activity receiving federal financial assistance." As a result of Title IX, the enrollment of women in athletics programs and professional schools increases dramatically.

How would that change our game?

WHAT ARE TWO ACTIVITIES THAT CAN BE USED TO TEACH AND LEARN MUSIC CONCEPTS?

Secondary

1. Building a Major Scale
   - All major scales in music have whole steps between them (two white keys on the piano that have a raised black key between them) except between the third and fourth and the seventh and eighth scale degrees.
     C—whole step—D—whole step—E—half step (no black key)— F—whole step—G—whole step—A—whole step—B—half step (no black key)—C
   - To represent these relationships kinesthetically, ask eight students to line up side by side and face the class. They will represent the most basic scale in music: C Major, with no sharps and no flats.
   - Have the first, second, and third persons (C, D, and E) stand one footstep apart.

○ The fourth person (F) should stand right next to the third person (E) because he or she represents a half step.
○ The fifth, sixth, and seventh persons (G, A, and B) stand one foot-step apart.
○ The eighth person (C) should stand right next to the seventh person (B) because he or she represents a half step. It will end up looking like this:

1st per	2nd per	3rd per	4th per	5th per	6th per	7th per	8th per
C	D	E	F	G	A	B	C

○ These relationships never change for any major key. When you start on a note other than C, you now need to use the black keys as a part of the scale, so those relationships are constant. For instance, a scale starting on G and ending on the next G has one sharp (a black key) in it—the F. The scale reads like this: G, A, B, C, D, E, F#, G.
○ To represent the sharp kinesthetically, have the F person stand on his or her toes and/or raise his or her arms in the air. When there are flats involved (the same black keys in different relationship), have the person either bend at the knees or at the waist. For instance, the key of F would be: F, G, A, Bb, C, D, E, F. If you work it out on a keyboard, both the key of F and G have a ½ step between the third and fourth scale degrees and the seventh and eighth scale degrees. You could practice on every major key if you'd like. This also works for the minor keys, but that is more advanced and the relationships are different. You could point this out to the music teachers in your class.

Secondary and Elementary

2. Chord Building
   ○ Ask eight students to line up side by side and face the class. They are going to represent a musical scale. In fact, they are going to represent a C Major scale, which is eight white keys in a row on the piano from one C to the next C.
   ○ Tell the students representing the scale that they are C, D, E, F, G, A, B, and C. You can hand them premade letter cards if you'd like.
   ○ Inform the C scale that they also represent a solfege scale (do-re-mi-fa-sol-la-ti-do), and sing it for them, pointing at each person as you move up the scale.
   ○ To build your first chord, have C, E, and G take one step forward. Those three people represent a I (one) chord in the key of C.

○ If you have the F, A, and C (in that order, the C is the high C) step forward, you have created a IV (four) chord in the key of C.

○ If you add one person to the end of the line (this person would be a D) and then have the G, B, and the new D person step forward, you have created a V (five chord) in the key of C.

○ These three chords represent the three keys used in blues music, and any musician could walk into a club and jam with fellow players on these three chords, literally, all night long. These three chords represent many other things as well.

WHAT ARE TWO ACTIVITIES THAT CAN BE USED TO TEACH AND LEARN ART CONCEPTS?

Elementary

1. The Secondary Spin—Reviewing primary colors and learning secondary colors
   ○ Ask students to match up with a partner.
   ○ Give them three pieces of colored construction paper. The paper should be the primary colors: red, blue, and yellow.
   ○ The teacher will shout out one of the secondary colors (orange, green, or violet).
   ○ Each group will have to quickly decide which two primary colors mixed together will make up the secondary color.
   ○ They will then hold up the primary colors, grab elbows, and begin to spin. The swinging represents the mixing of the colors to form the secondary color.
   ○ You can add a little more excitement and ask participants to see if they can be one of the fastest groups to find the primary colors and start their spin.
   ○ The intermediate colors can also be taught through this exercise if you would like (red-violet, red-orange, yellow-orange, yellow-green, blue-green, and blue-violet).

Secondary

2. Symmetrical and Asymmetrical Art—Creating symmetrical and asymmetrical designs with bodies as the only material source
   ○ The teacher will define and describe the difference between symmetrical and asymmetrical art. The teacher may also consider the idea of placing some examples on an overhead or hanging them around the room.
   ○ At this point, the teacher will put students in groups of six to 10.

- Students will be given 10 minutes to create symmetrical and asymmetrical designs with their group members.
- The only materials that they can use are their bodies (standing or lying down).
- After 10 minutes, each group will come to the front of the room to show one symmetrical shape and one asymmetrical shape. The class will differentiate between the two. Encourage your participants to be creative and have fun.

WHAT ARE TWO ACTIVITIES THAT CAN BE USED TO TEACH AND LEARN HEALTH CONCEPTS?

Elementary

1. Fruits and Vegetables Tag—Learning the dietary importance of fruits and vegetables
   - The teacher will set up boundaries for the game.
   - Students will play the role of germs and disease by speed walking around the designated area. They will try to avoid being tagged by the fruits and vegetables.
   - The teacher will choose one or two students (depending on class size) to be a fruit or a vegetable. For example, a person holding a red ball may be a tomato.
   - The fruits and vegetables chase the germs and disease. Once they tag them, they are dead, and they come out of the game.
   - During the first round, the teacher will time the fruits and vegetables to see how long it takes them to kill the germs and disease.
   - After each round is played, the teacher will add another fruit or vegetable to the game. The time it takes the fruits and vegetables to kill the germs and disease will get faster and faster.
   - Note: The more fruits and vegetables in your diet, the better chance your body has of fighting off germs and disease.

Secondary

2. The Insulin Sweep—Understanding the sugar-insulin relationship and insulin resistance relationship
   - Line up two rows of four or five chairs directly across from each other, creating a small aisle between them.
   - Line up the same number of students (as chairs), single file at the entrance of the aisle.
   - One other student, with a broom, should line up at the other end of the aisle, facing the line of students.

- Have the line of participants walk, very slowly, into the aisle (bloodstream) toward the student with the broom (insulin).
- The broom student yells, "Hey, there's sugar in the bloodstream," and begins walking toward the line of participants, sweeping his or her broom across the floor.
- As the broom meets the feet of the students in line, they should be seated in an open seat (cell).
- Point out the job of insulin in this oversimplified model. Insulin is sweeping the bloodstream clear of sugar into cells for energy use.
- The next step is to have students bounce off the chairs, move back into the aisle, and swim around, even though the sweeping is going on (insulin resistance leading to continued abundances of sugar in the blood and the possibility of weight gain, obesity, and type 2 diabetes).
- Repeat as necessary to include some or all of the participants!

CHAPTER SUMMARY

- Read all movement activities in this chapter because you never know what information will trigger a creative thought in your brain.
- Education is cross curricular with a strong spiral profile.
- The goal of this chapter is to inspire your creative process about how your content can be taught through movement.
- Allow your perspective to broaden as you consider everything you teach. With some thought and planning, you can build on these ideas and make them fit your needs.
- Teaching and learning through movement is well worth the time it takes to develop and perfect.
- These activities can accompany or replace what you are already doing in the classroom.
- Eight movement activities that can be used to teach and learn language arts concepts are (1) Word Hop, (2) Country Versus City, (3) The Syllable Slide, (4) Peer Editing Hop, (5) Sentence Relay, (6) The Fit Factor Decision, (7) Transition Word Scramble, and (8) Colon-Semi Fist Bump.
- Eight movement activities that can be used to teach and learn math concepts are (1) The Even/Odd Hop, (2) Counting in Action, (3) Ascending and Descending Birthday, (4) The Integer Dance, (5) Human Box-and-Whiskers Plots, (6) Destroyer: Systems of Equations Review, (7) Simon Says, Parent Graph Edition, and (8) People Graphing.
- Eight movement activities that can be used to teach and learn science concepts are (1) Biomes, (2) Magnet Tag, (3) Conduction, Convection, Ra-Ra Radiation, (4) Density, (5) Human Diffusion,

(6) Electricity: That's How It Flows, (7) Mole Conversion Activity/ Physical Phenceposting, and (8) The Body Systems.

- Eight movement activities that can be used to teach and learn social studies concepts are (1) Money and Making a Dollar, (2) Marketing, Bartering, and Negotiating, (3) The Human Map, (4) Hands Across America, (5) Trench Warfare, (6) The American Industrial Revolution, (7) The Plague, and (8) Unhappy Baseball.
- Two movement activities that can be used to teach music concepts are (1) Building a Major Scale and (2) Chord Building.
- Two movement activities to teach and learn art concepts are (1) The Secondary Spin and (2) Symmetrical and Asymmetrical Art.
- Two movement activities to teach and learn health concepts are (1) Fruits and Vegetables Tag and (2) The Insulin Sweep.

TIPS FOR THE STAFF DEVELOPER

Be sure to have teachers experience a wide variety of these activities, so they understand that they are applicable for all content areas and grade levels. Ask the question, "Could a student teach this at home tonight?" The answer is almost always yes. Also be sure to remind teachers that these activities are how the brain prefers to learn and how they make the teaching process more efficient as they spend less time reteaching a concept. Finally, suggest that when teachers use this type of teaching, students are given the opportunity to put the content to "paper and pencil." Ultimately, students will be assessed this way, not through using their bodies. They must practice transitioning in their brain from the procedural lane to the semantic lane.

References and Resources

Blaydes Madigan, J. (1999). *Thinking on your feet*. Murphy, TX: Action Based Learning.

Blaydes Madigan, J., & Hess, C. (2004). *Action based learning lab manual*. Murphy, TX: Action Based Learning.

Blom, L. C., Alvarez, J., Zhang, L., & Kolbo, J. (2011). Associations between health-related physical fitness, academic achievement and selected academic behaviors of elementary and middle school students in the state of Mississippi. *ICHPER-SD Journal of Research, 6*(1), 28–34.

Brage, S., Ekelund, U., Haapala, E. A., Laaka, T., Lintu, N., Poikkeus, A., . . . Westgate, K. (2016). Physical activity and sedentary time in relation to academic achievement in children. *Journal of Science and Medicine in Sport.* Retrieved from http://dx.doi.org/10.1016/j.jsams.2016.11.003

Braniff, C. (2011). Perceptions of an active classroom: Exploration of movement and collaboration with fourth grade students. *Networks.* Retrieved from http://journals.library.wisc.edu/index.php/networks/article/view/413/459

Bruer, J. T. (1991). The brain and child development: Time for some critical thinking. *Public Health Reports, 113*(5), 388–397.

Burr, S. (2009). The effect of kinesthetic teaching techniques on student learning (Unpublished master's thesis). Gratz College, Melrose Park, PA.

Dennison, P. E., & Dennison, G. (1988). Brain gym, teachers edition. Ventura, CA: Edu-Kinesthetics.

Donnelly, J., & Lambourne, K. (2011). Classroom-based physical activity, cognition, and academic achievement. *Preventive Medicine, 52*, S3–S42.

Firth, J., Richards, J., Rosenbaum, S., Schuch, F. B., Sui, X., Stubbs, B., . . . Ward, P. B. (2016). Are lower levels of cardiorespiratory fitness associated with incident depression? A systematic review of prospective cohort studies, *Preventive Medicine, 93*, 159–165.

Fox. M. (2006, February 5). Betty Friedan, who ignited cause in "feminine Mystique," dies at 85. *New York Times.* Retrieved from http://www.nytimes.com/2006/02/05/us/betty-friedan-who-ignited-cause-in-feminine-mystique-dies-at-85.html

Gibbs, S. (2009). Using bodily-kinesthetic activities to foster student success in a high school Spanish classroom (Unpublished master's thesis). Gratz College, Melrose Park, PA.

Glasser, W. (1998). *Choice theory: A new psychology for personal freedom*. New York, NY: HarperCollins.

Hamilton, M. (2008). Too little exercise and too much sitting: Inactivity physiology and the need for new recommendations on sedentary behavior. *Current Cardiovascular Risk Reports, 2*(4), 292–298.

Hannaford, C. (1995). *Smart moves: Why learning is not all in the head.* Marshall, NC: Great Ocean.

Healy, J. (1990). *Endangered minds: Why our children don't think, and what to do about it.* New York, NY: Touchstone Rockefeller Center.

Heinrich, L., & Gullone, E. (2006). The clinical significance of loneliness. A literature review. *Clinical Psychology Review, 26*(6), 695–718.

Hubbard, J. (2009). Kinesthetic mathematics instruction for secondary students with traumatic brain injury (Unpublished master's thesis). Gratz College, Melrose Park, PA.

Jensen, E. (1998). *Teaching with the brain in mind.* Alexandria, VA: Association for Supervision and Curriculum Development.

Jensen, E. (2000). *Learning with the body in mind.* San Diego, CA: The Brain Store.

KidsHealth. (2015). Why exercise is wise. KidsHealth.org, author. Retrieved from http://kidshealth.org/en/teens/exercise-wise.html?ref=search

Kinoshita, H. (1997). Run for your brain's life. *Brain Work, 7*(1), 8.

Kissler, A. (1994). *On course: Games for everyone.* Auburn, CA: On Course.

Kluger, J. (2012). We never talk anymore: The problem with text messaging. Mobile Tech Special. *Time.* Retrieved from http://techland.time.com/2012/08/16/we-never-talk-anymore-the-problem-with-text-messaging/

Konigs, M., Oosterlaan, J., Scherder, E., & Verbeurgh, L. (2014). Physical exercise and executive functions in preadolescent children, adolescents and young adults: A meta-analysis, *British Journal of Sports Medicine, 48*(12), 973–979.

Lengel, T., & Kuczala, M. (2010). *The kinesthetic classroom: Teaching and learning through movement.* Thousand Oaks, CA: Corwin.

Medina, J. (2008). *Brain rules.* Seattle, WA: Pear Press.

Mitchell, M. (2009). *Physical activity may strengthen children's ability to pay attention.* University of Illinois at Urbana-Champaign: News Bureau.

Oberparleiter, L. (2004). *Brain-based teaching and learning.* Department of Education, Gratz College. Graduate Course Trainers Manual. Randolph, NJ: Center for Lifelong Learning.

Oberparleiter, L. (2011). *The role of emotion and reflection in student achievement.* Bloomington, IN: Authorhouse.

Ormrod, J. E. (2014). *Education psychology: Developing learners.* Boston, MA: Pearson.

Owen, N., Healy, G. N., Matthews, C. E., & Dunstan, D. W. (2010). Too much sitting: The population health science of sedentary behavior. *Exercise and Sport Sciences Reviews, 38*(3), 105–113.

Pica, R. (2006). *A running start: How play, physical activity, and free time create a successful child.* New York, NY: Marlowe and Company.

Promislow, S. (1999). *Making the brain-body connection: A playful guide to releasing mental, physical, and emotional blocks to success.* Vancouver, BC, Canada: Kinetic.

Putnam, S. C. (2003, February). Attention deficit: Medical or environmental disorder? *Principal Leadership, 3*(6), 59–61.

Queen, A. J., & Queen, P. S. (2004). *The frazzled teacher's wellness plan: A five-step program for reclaiming time, managing stress, and creating a healthy lifestyle.* Thousand Oaks, CA: Corwin.

Radiological Society of North America. (2016, November 30). Aerobic exercise preserves brain volume and improves cognitive function. *ScienceDaily*. Retrieved from http://www.sciencedaily.com/releases/2016/11/161130130916.htm

Ratey, J. (2008). *SPARK: The revolutionary new science of exercise and the brain*. New York, NY: Little, Brown and Company.

Schmitt, B. D. (1999). *Your child's health: The parents' one-stop reference guide to symptoms, emergencies, common illnesses, behavior problems and healthy development*. New York, NY: Bantam Books.

Shade, R. A. (1996). *License to laugh: Humor in the classroom*. Westport, CT: Teachers Idea Press.

Sousa, D. (2017). *How the brain learns*. Thousand Oaks, CA: Corwin.

Sprenger, M. (1999). *Learning and memory: The brain in action*. Alexandria, VA: Association for Supervision and Curriculum Development.

Stagman, S., & Cooper, J. L. (2010, April). Children's mental health: What every policymaker should know. National Center for Children in Poverty. Retrieved from http://www.nccp.org/publications/pdf/text_929.pdf

Sternberg, E., & Gold, P. (2002). The mind-body interaction in disease: The hidden mind [Special edition]. *Scientific American, 12*(1), 82–129.

Sullo, B. (2007). *Activating the desire to learn*. Alexandria, VA: Association for Supervision and Curriculum Development.

Sylwester R. (1995). *A celebration of neurons: An educator's guide to the human brain*. Alexandria, VA: Association for Supervision and Curriculum Development.

Texas Education Agency. (2009). *Overview*. Retrieved from http://www.cooperinstitute.org/ourkidshealth/documents/Data%200verview—3-9-09.pdf

U.S. Department of Health and Human Services, Centers for Disease Control and Prevention, National Center for Chronic Disease Prevention and Health Promotion, Division of Adolescent and School Health. (2010, July). *The association between school-based physical activity, including physical education, and academic performance*. Retrieved from https://www.cdc.gov/healthyyouth/health_and_academics/pdf/pa-pe_paper.pdf

Winterfeld, A. (2007). PE makes a comeback. *State Legislatures Magazine, 33*(10), 36–37.

Wood, N. (2009). *The impact of movement on the student's ability to retain information* (Unpublished master's thesis). Gratz College, Melrose Park, PA.

Wooten Green, A. (2016). Physical education and recess improve behavior, test scores. *Carolina Parent*. Retrieved from http://www.carolinaparent.com/Physical-Education-and-Recess-Improve-Behavior-Test-Scores/

Yarcheski, A., Mahon, E., & Yarcheski, T. (2011, June). Stress, hope, and loneliness in young adolescents. *Psychological Reports, 108*(3), 919–922.

Index

CORWIN HAS ONE MISSION: to enhance education through intentional professional learning.

We build long-term relationships with our authors, educators, clients, and associations who partner with us to develop and continuously improve the best evidence-based practices that establish and support lifelong learning.

OUR MISSION: Changing the future for all children, by increasing their health, wellness and education through movement.

Solutions you want. Experts you trust. Results you need.